Contents

PHYSICAL GEOGRAPHY

Coastal landscapes 1
- Coastal landscapes as systems 1
- Physical factors influencing coastal landscape systems 1
- Development of coastal landforms 2
- Coastal sediment sources 2
- Formation of erosional landforms 3
- Formation of depositional landforms 3
- Case study – high and low energy coastlines 3
- Emergent and submergent coastal landscapes 4
- Case study – human activity affecting coastal landscapes 4
- Case study – economic development affecting coastal landscapes 4

Glaciated landscapes 5
- Glaciated landscapes as systems 5
- Physical factors affecting glaciated landscapes 5
- Types of glaciers and glacier movement 5
- Development of glaciated landforms 6
- Glacio-fluvial landforms and climate change 7
- Case study – inter-related glaciated landforms 7
- Periglacial landforms and climate change 7
- Case study – human activity affecting periglacial landscapes .. 7

Dryland landscapes 8
- Dryland landscapes as systems 8
- Physical factors influencing dryland landscapes 8
- Types of drylands 8
- Development of dryland landscapes 9
- Case study – inter-related dry landscapes 9
- Periglacial landforms resulting from colder periods 10
- Case study – water supply issues in dryland landscapes 10

Water and carbon cycles 11
- Importance of water and carbon systems for life on Earth 11
- Water cycle 11
- Carbon cycle 11
- Case study – tropical rainforests and Arctic tundra 12
- Human factors affecting water and carbon processes and stores 13
- Pathways and processes controlling water and carbon cycles .. 13
- Interdependence of water and carbon cycles 14
- Global implications of water and carbon management 14

Exploring oceans 15
- Oceans as a distinctive feature of the Earth 15
- Factors influencing ocean biodiversity 15
- Use of ocean energy and mineral resources 15
- Governing the oceans and resource management 16
- Pollutants affecting ocean systems 16
- Case study – dangers of offshore oil production 16
- Climate change affecting oceans 17
- Case study – threats to island communities 17
- Globalisation of oceans 17

Hazardous Earth 18
- Global distribution of tectonic hazards 18
- Tectonic plate boundaries 18
- Theories of continental drift and plate tectonics 19
- Coping with risks of tectonic hazards 19
- Volcanic activity and resultant landforms 20
- Managing volcanic hazards 20
- Earthquake activity and resultant landforms 21
- Managing earthquake hazards 21
- Responses to volcanic activity 22
- Responses to earthquake activity 22

Climate change 23
- Historic changes in Earth's climate 23
- Natural forces that have influenced climate change 23
- The Anthropocene 24
- Responses to climate change 24
- Impacts of climate change 25
- Mitigation and adaptation in response to climate change 25

Miralo Education Group Ltd owner of SnapRevise® trademark, 6 Cranwell Road, Locking Parklands, Weston-super-Mare, BS24 7G, United Kingdom
Copyright © Miralo Education Group 2026, Published by Miralo Education Group Ltd CN 15550989
All rights reserved. These notes are protected by copyright owned by Miralo Education Group Ltd ("Publishers") and you may not reproduce, disseminate, or communicate to the public the whole or a substantial part thereof except as permitted at law or with the prior written consent of Miralo Education Group Ltd.
Title: A-Level Geography Summary Notes
ISBN: 978-1-918046-01-4

Disclaimer: No reliance on warranty. These SnapRevise materials are intended to supplement but are not intended to replace or to be any substitute for your regular school attendance, for referring to prescribed texts, or for your own note taking. You are responsible for following the appropriate syllabus, attending school classes, and maintaining good study practices. It is your responsibility to evaluate the accuracy of any information, opinions, and advice in these materials. Under no circumstance will Miralo Education Group Ltd ("Publishers"), their officers, agents, or employees be liable for any loss or damage caused by your use or reliance on these materials, including any adverse impact upon your performance in any academic subject as a result of your use or reliance on the materials. You accept that all information provided or made available by the Publishers is in the nature of general information and does not constitute advice. It is not guaranteed to be error-free and you should always independently verify any information, including through use of a professional teacher and other reliable resources. To the extent permissible at law, the Publishers expressly disclaim all warranties or guarantees of any kind, whether express or implied, including without limitation any warranties concerning the accuracy or content of information provided in these materials or other fitness for purpose. The Publishers shall not be liable for any direct, indirect, special, incidental, consequential or punitive damages of any kind. You agree to indemnify the Publishers, its officers, employees, and agents against any loss whatsoever by using these materials.

Contents

HUMAN GEOGRAPHY

Changing spaces and places 26
    Place identity and perception. 26
    Factors influencing perceptions of place 26
    Distribution of resources, wealth, and opportunities across places 27
    Placemaking process of rebranding 27
    Social inequality and structural economic change 27
    The effect of cyclic economic change on social inequality 28
    People influencing places 28

International trade and globalisation 29
    International trade flows and patterns. 29
    Human Development Index 29
    Effects of international trade 29
    Factors influencing access to markets. 30
    Case study – interdependence between trading partners 30

Global migration 31
    Global migration flows and patterns. 31
    Factors influencing global migration patterns 32
    Effects of global migration 32
    Case study – migration corridors. 33
    Case study – opportunities and challenges of migration 33

Power and borders 34
    Sovereign nation states 34
    Factors challenging sovereignty and territorial integrity 34
    Case study – challenges to sovereignty 34
    Global governance and responding to conflict 35
    Global to local cooperation 35
    Global governance of sovereignty and territorial integrity 35

Health and disease 36
    Classification and patterns of disease 36
    Factors affecting the prevalence of disease. 36
    Case study – natural hazards affecting disease spread 36
    Trends in communicable and non-communicable diseases 37
    Case study – disease causes and response strategies 37
    Increasing global mobility affecting diffusion of disease 38
    Nature as a source of medicines 38
    Strategies for disease risk and eradication 38

Food security 39
    Variations in patterns of food security. 39
    Theoretical positions on food security. 39
    Global food production system. 39
    Feeding the world's population. 39
    Effects of globalisation on the food industry 40
    Factors influencing food security. 40
    Risks to food security 41
    Impacts on the food system 41
    Imbalance in the global food system. 42
    Food as a geopolitical commodity 42
    Strategies to improve food security 42

Human rights 43
    Global variation in human rights norms 43
    Factors influencing patterns of human rights violations. 43
    Geography of gender inequality 43
    Human rights violations as a consequence of conflict 44
    Global governance of human rights 44
    Case study – human rights governance 44
    Consequences of global governance of human rights 44

Coastal landscapes

Coastal landscapes as systems

Coastal landscapes are **open systems**, meaning energy can be transferred in and out:

Inputs	• Deposition of sediments (from rivers, cliffs, offshore) • Kinetic energy from waves/wind; thermal energy from sun • Material from mass movement and weathering
Processes	• Transportation through longshore drift, traction, saltation, solution, suspension, and deposition of sediments • Mechanical, chemical and biological weathering • Erosion – hydraulic action, abrasion, solution, attrition
Stores	• Beaches, spits, onshore bars, tombolos, and seabed sediment
Outputs	• Sand blown from wind erosion • Sediment lost from erosion or offshore deposition

Coasts naturally fall into a **dynamic equilibrium** where the balance between inputs and outputs are equal over time despite short term imbalances. Long term imbalances such as rising sea levels and extreme weather due to climate change or human management methods such as groynes can have damaging effects on this equilibrium.

- **Sediment budget:** the difference between the volume of sediment that enters the coastline and the volume that leaves. A positive budget means the coastline grows; a negative budget means the coastline retreats.
- **Sediment cells:** sections of the coastline that form closed systems within the larger coastline. This means material stays within each cell and is rarely interrupted by other cells. Natural landforms such as headlands and bays usually act as the boundaries for each cell, preventing movement of sediment between them. England and Wales have 11 sediment cells (shown on the right), each containing smaller sub-cells.

Physical factors influencing coastal landscape systems

Coasts are affected by five main physical factors:
- **Wind:** provides lots of energy for coastal processes.
  ◦ Higher wind speeds transfer more energy to waves, causing them to be larger and more destructive.
  ◦ Wind direction determines the direction of longshore drift.
  ◦ High wind frequency causes more erosive waves and allows for more sediment transportation.
- **Waves:** form due to the friction created by wind blowing over the water surface. Stronger winds create steeper waves.
  ◦ **Swash:** water moving up the beach
  ◦ **Backwash:** water moving back down the beach once losing energy
  ◦ **Constructive waves:** low waves, long wavelength, strong swash, and push sediment onto the beach without removing any. They build gentle beach profiles.
  ◦ **Destructive waves:** high waves, short wavelength, weak swash, and strong backwash that removes sediment from beaches. They build steep beach profiles.
- **Tides:** are a result of the gravitational pull of the sea towards and from the Moon and Sun, causing the regular rise and fall of sea level.

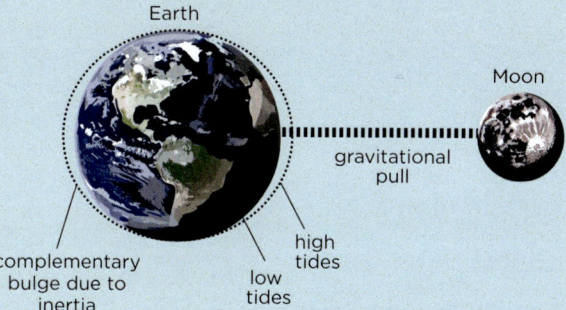

  ◦ High tides occur when the Sun and Moon are aligned so the gravitational pull is stronger.
  ◦ Coasts with larger tidal ranges (larger difference between low and high tide) are more vulnerable to erosion.
- **Geology:**
  ◦ **Lithology** refers to the type and characteristics of rocks. Hard, resistant rocks such as granite experience a slow rate of erosion. Softer rock like clay erodes much faster due to its weak chemical composition.
  ◦ Structure refers to the arrangement of rocks. **Concordant coastlines** form when rock layers are parallel to the coast. **Discordant coastlines** form when the layers are perpendicular to the coast resulting in headlands and bays.
- **Ocean currents:**
  ◦ The movement of water around the globe impacts coastal processes.
  ◦ Warmer currents can transfer more energy and cause more erosion than colder currents. They also cause more evaporation and precipitation which links to chemical weathering.
  ◦ Rip currents are fast flowing and can quickly remove sediment.
  ◦ Longshore currents transport sediment along the coastline.

Coastal landscapes

Development of coastal landforms

Types of weathering affecting development of coastal landforms		
Mechanical/physical	**Chemical**	**Biological**
• **Freeze thaw:** water fills small cracks in rock, freezes, and expands as ice which widens the crack, over time leading to rockfalls. • **Salt crystallisation:** saltwater enters cracks in rocks, then evaporates leaving salt crystals. The cycle repeats causing build up that expands the cracks. • **Thermal expansion:** rocks expand when warm and contract when cool. Repeated cycles can cause them to crack and break off.	• **Carbonation:** rainwater absorbs atmospheric carbon dioxide forming weak carbonic acid that reacts with and dissolves certain types of rock. • **Oxidation:** oxygen in the atmosphere or water reacts with iron-rich rock and forms rust, weakening the rock and making it more prone to rockfall. • **Hydration:** water chemically reacts with rock minerals, causing the surface to weaken and flake away.	• **Plant roots:** roots can grow into cracks of rock, forcing them open and weakening the cliff. This occurs most significantly on cliff tops. Burrowing animals can have a similar impact. • **Organic acids:** small plants like moss and lichen can produce acids that react with rock and dissolve it.

- **Mass movement** is when gravitational force outweighs the upwards force of material, causing it to collapse. Examples include:
  - **Rockfalls:** weathered rock breaks off the cliff face, landing at the base where it is most likely washed away.
  - **Slumping:** heavy rainfall means soft rock becomes saturated with water making it heavier and causing it to slip downwards.
  - **Landslides:** usually occur when a layer of rock or bedding becomes loose causing large slabs of material to slide down slip planes when weakened.
- **Wave processes:** there are several types of erosion, all of which contribute to the formation of landforms such as wave-cut platforms, arches, caves and stacks. These include:
  - **Hydraulic action:** waves force air and water into cracks and pores in rock causing the cracks to expand and break apart over time.
  - **Attrition:** rocks colliding with each other, breaking them into smaller and smoother pieces.
  - **Abrasion:** sediment in waves rubs against cliffs slowly wearing it away.
  - **Solution:** certain rocks such as limestone and chalk erode as they dissolve in water.
- **Transportation:** deposition of sediments once they are transported helps to form landforms such as spits, bars and tombolos. When material no longer has a source of energy for transportation, it slows down and accumulates. For example, during the backwash of constructive waves or in low energy environments such as river estuaries.
  - **Solution:** minerals from rocks dissolved and carried in the water.
  - **Suspension:** fine particles are carried by the water's current.
  - **Saltation:** small sediment like sand or pebbles are pushed and bounce along the seabed.
  - **Traction:** large rocks roll along the sea floor due to the energy transferred from the underwater tides and currents.
- **Fluvial processes:** fluvial erosion occurs towards the mouth of a river where sediment for the coastline is largely supplied. This sediment is transported by solution, suspension, saltation, or traction before being deposited at the mouth where energy is much lower (e.g. the Mississippi Delta was formed because of the rate of material input exceeds the rate of output where the river meets the ocean). This is amplified by **flocculation** where clay particles are electrically attracted to each other and form clumps in saltwater.
- **Aeolian processes:** 'aeolian' refers to wind. Strong winds are capable of eroding sandy landscapes in a process called deflation, where loose sand particles are picked up and moved by saltation. These particles are often transported inland where they accumulate to form sand dunes once wind speed drops.

Coastal sediment sources

Coastal sediment can be supplied from a range of terrestrial, offshore, and human sources.

- **Terrestrial sources:**
  - **Fluvial deposition:** rivers provide the coastline with sediment. This helps to maintain the dynamic equilibrium and adds to the sediment budget.
  - **Weathering and mass movement:** mechanical, biological, and chemical weathering loosens rock making it more likely to collapse. Mass movements such as landslides and rockfalls provide large volumes of material to the coastline which can then be transported.
  - **Marine erosion:** waves erode cliffs, adding lots of sediment to the coastline. Extreme weather and storms increase wave energy which causes faster erosion, particularly where rock is weakened or soft.
  - **Aeolian deposition:** wind picks up and transports fine sediment particles like sand and deposits them at landforms such as beaches and sand dunes.
  - **Longshore drift:** when waves meet the shore at an angle, sediment is transported along the coast in swash and is carried downwards perpendicular to the beach.
- **Offshore sources:** marine deposition occurs when tidal action and constructive waves transport material from the seabed towards the shore. This can help to form landforms such as spits.
- **Human sources:** when there is a **negative sediment budget,** beach nourishment is used to replace sediment that is lost to erosion. It is commonly done by dredging material offshore from the seabed or by sourcing it elsewhere and dumping it onto the beach from a truck. Sea defences such as groynes can also cause sediment accumulation at a certain section of the coastline due to human intervention.

Coastal landscapes

Formation of erosional landforms
- **Headlands and bays:** these landforms are usually found along discordant coastlines, where alternating bands of hard and soft rock are perpendicular to the coastline.
  - Differential erosion: the bands of softer rock erode faster forming bays, while the harder rocks are more resistant, so they form headlands.
  - They are much less likely to form along concordant coastlines, as resistant rock usually lays parallel to the coastline, however weaknesses in geology can allow for small coves and bays to form (e.g. Dorset coast).
- **Caves, arches, stacks, and stumps:** these landforms represent processes that often occur along headlands.
  1. Cracks form in the cliff due to weathering processes and hydraulic action.
  2. The crack grows larger over time forming a cave on one side of the headland.
  3. The cave becomes deeper due to abrasion and eventually pushes through to the other side of the headland forming an arch.
  4. Continued erosion and chemical weathering over time causes the arch to collapse, leaving a tall stack of rock.
  5. Being exposed to wave action and erosion eventually causes the stack to fall, leaving behind a smaller stump of rock (e.g. Old Harry rocks, Dorset).

soft rock (more eroded, retreats over time e.g. clay, sand)
hard rock (less eroded, juts out over time e.g. chalk, limestone)

- **Cliffs and wave-cut platforms:**
  - When waves attack the base of a cliff, undercutting occurs due to hydraulic action and abrasion. This leaves an overhang of rock above the wave-cut notch.
  - Over time, the cliff is no longer supported so it collapses and retreats. Repeated undercutting leaves a gently sloping shore platform.
- **Geos:**
  - Geos are deep, narrow inlets in the side of a cliff, formed when an initial weakness or crack in rock is repeatedly attacked by waves, hydraulic action, and abrasion.
  - Repeated erosion deepens the inlet inland creating a deep channel.
  - They sometimes begin as long, narrow caves until the roof collapses and forms a geo (e.g. Calder's Geo, Scotland).
- **Blowholes:**
  - Blowholes are like geos, however they form when only part of the tunnel roof collapses along a weakened joint in the rock. This leaves a hole in the cliff top that sprays water upwards during stormy conditions.

Formation of depositional landforms
- **Beaches:** form when sediment accumulates from deposition by constructive waves, rivers, eroded material or human inputs like beach nourishment. Storms and strong destructive waves can rapidly remove large volumes of material from beaches, leaving short beach profiles.
  - **Berms** are ridges formed by deposition at each high tide.
  - **Cusps** are curved marks in the beach showing the indentations caused by waves.
- **Spits:** are long extensions of the coastline that form because of longshore drift acting in a direction of open water such as an estuary or bay (e.g. sandbanks). Over time, repeated deposition of sediment means the spit grows in length.
  - **Recurved spits** can have a hooked end due to wave refraction. The area behind them is a sheltered, low energy environment that can become a salt marsh.
  - **Onshore bars:** are spits that extend across a bay, connecting two headlands (e.g. Slapton Sands, Devon). This leaves a lagoon of trapped brackish water behind it.
- **Salt marshes:** form in low energy environments when sediments such as silt and clay are deposited in large volumes and flocculation occurs, forming mudflats. They then experience vegetative succession where salt tolerant plants colonise the area.
- **Tombolos:** are extensions of land that can join islands to mainland, forming from longshore drift transporting sediment offshore and depositing it where wave refraction occurs.

Case study – high and low energy coastlines

	Holderness, UK (high energy coastline)	Rhône Delta, France (low energy coastline)
Key details	• Located along the east coast of England, the Holderness coastline extends 60 kilometres from Flamborough Head to Saltburn.	• Located in Southern France where the mouth of the Rhône River meets the Mediterranean Sea.
Landforms	• Discordant coastline featuring headlands and bays. • At Flamborough Head, resistant rock means wavecut platforms, caves, and arches have formed. • In bays, slumping of cliffs occurs and the transporting of loose sediment forms a recurved spit due to longshore drift known as Spurn Point.	• Longshore drift has created several onshore bars and spits. • Behind these landforms, salt marshes and lagoons form. • Mainly comprised of narrow beaches with occasional sand dunes.
Physical factors affecting the landscape	• In Holderness, weak boulder clays form bays, and chalk forms headlands. Weathering processes also impact landforms and their appearance. • Strong prevailing winds produce destructive waves causing rapid erosion and transportation of sediment.	• High deposition rate, flocculation, and sediment from the Alps has developed the delta over 7,000 years. • Small tidal range of 30cm means weak currents and little exposure to erosion.
Changes to the coastline over time	• One of the fastest eroding coastlines in the world of an average 2m retreat every year. • 200 homes have been lost into the sea due to the rapid erosion and weak geology of bays.	• Changes seasonally, with salt marshes flooded during spring and winter. • Longshore drift, spits, and bars have developed over a long period of time.

Coastal landscapes

Emergent and submergent coastal landscapes
- Changes in sea level can be caused by:
  - **Eustatic changes:** increase or decrease in the volume of water affecting sea level (e.g. more water when ice melts after a glacial period).
  - **Isostatic changes:** rise or fall in land level relative to sea level (e.g. post-glacial rebound after ice melts).
- **Emergent landforms** form when a fall in sea level exposes the seabed. Examples of emergent landforms include:
  - **Raised beaches:** former wave-cut platforms and beaches now lying above current sea level due to uplift or sea level drop. These are often composed of sand, shingle, and marine sediments, sometimes with fossil shells (e.g. Isle of Arran, Scotland).
  - **Abandoned cliffs:** are former cliff faces left inland after the sea retreats due to falling sea levels or land uplift. These have features like notches, caves, or wave-cut benches no longer covered by waves. They may be vegetated or degraded over time by sub-aerial processes (e.g. weathering, mass movement).
  - **Marine terraces:** are stepped coastal platforms formed by wave erosion at former sea levels, then uplifted or exposed by sea level fall. Multiple terraces indicate successive stillstands or pauses in sea level change so are useful for reconstructing past sea levels.

During historic changes in climate such as during glacial periods, global temperatures were much lower meaning ice coverage was higher, and the sea level was lower. Other changes (e.g. melting glaciers) also lowers sea levels as pressure is relieved from the land which was previously weighed down, meaning the land rises relative to sea level.

- **Submergent** landforms form when there is an increase in sea level. This can occur when increasing global temperatures causes ice to melt, raising relative sea level. Thermal expansion of oceans also increases the volume of water and subsequent sea levels. Examples of submergent landforms include:
  - **Rias:** submerged river valleys. When sea levels rise, these valleys flood, leaving only the highest parts of the valley sides exposed. These mainly occur around the estuaries of river valleys, though previous tributaries and river channels are still evident underwater (e.g. Kingsbury Estuary, UK).
  - **Fjords:** submerged glacial U-shaped valleys with steep sides due to high rates of erosion at the basin. They have shallower sections at the sea end due to lower rates of erosion as ice there was thinner when it melted (e.g. Lysefjord, Norway).
  - **Shingle beaches:** when sea levels were much lower during glacial periods, sediment was deposited along the land. As this land became submerged, wave action pushed and transported this sediment inland, forming beaches and tombolos (e.g. Chesil Beach, Dorset).
- Around 20,000 years ago, Earth was experiencing a glacial period, so much more water was stored as ice. During the post-glacial period, water stored in ice sheets began to be released as it melted causing a eustatic rise in sea level. In the current interglacial period (Holocene) warming continues, and sea level is still rising with the influence of global warming and climate change.

Case study – human activity affecting coastal landscapes

	Sandbanks, Dorset
Key details	• The properties along the coastline are highly valuable due to demand, with one home selling for £13.5 million. • The Sandbanks beach also attract tourists that boosts the local economy. • Intervention is necessary at the end of the spit to prevent longshore drift from blocking the entrance to Poole Harbour.
Management strategy	• Beach nourishment is used to ensure a positive sediment budget and maintain wide beaches. • Rock groynes are used to interrupt longshore drift and trap sediment.
Consequences of these strategies	• Wider beaches have been created with a gently sloping profile to ensure the tourist attraction and landscape is maintained. • Rock groynes also protect the beach from erosion. • Implementation of these strategies is very costly and the structures must be replenished or replaced over time.

Case study – economic development affecting coastal landscapes

	Mangawhai to Pākiri, New Zealand
Key details	• For over 70 years, sand mining has occurred off the Mangawhai to Pakiri coastline, north of Aukland. • The sand is high quality with a high silica content, so is useful for construction, beach nourishment, and glass production. • Approximately 75,000 cubic metres of sand is mined each year.
Impacts	• Offshore sand removal starves the beach of sediment, leading to a lower/flatter beach profile and weaker defences against wave erosion. • Dredging also removes sediment from the sediment budget, disturbing the nature of sediment cells. • Loss of dunes and vegetation exposes underlying rock and clay. • This has led to coastal retreat and erosion posing risks for people and buildings further inland as the likelihood of floods increases. • Dunes and wide beaches that once acted as buffers from storm waves have been diminished. • The Mangawhai spit is more vulnerable to storm breaching, altering tidal flows into the nearby estuary. • Ongoing sediment deficit means beaches may not naturally recover.

Glaciated landscapes

All specs except: CIE, Pearson IAL

Glaciated landscapes as systems
Glacier landscapes are **open systems**, meaning energy can be transferred in and out:

Inputs	• Deposition of sediments • Kinetic energy from wind and glacial movement • Thermal energy from the sun • Material from mass movement, weathering, snow accumulation
Processes	• Movement of glaciers and transportation of debris • Deposition of sediments • Mechanical, chemical and biological weathering • Insolation (solar radiation)
Stores	• Ice mass, water, and material held by glaciers
Outputs	• Ablation and meltwater which evaporates into the atmosphere • Sublimation (direct formation of gaseous water vapour from ice

- Glaciated landscapes naturally fall into a **dynamic equilibrium** where the balance between inputs and outputs are mostly equal over time despite short term imbalances and variance. Long term imbalances such as climate change or human activity can have damaging effects on this equilibrium.
- **Glacier mass balance:** the difference between the volume of snow and ice that is added to the glaciers and the volume that leaves via ablation. A positive budget enables growth of a glacier; a negative budget means a glacier retreats.
  ◦ When ablation = accumulation, no growth occurs.
  ◦ The upper region of glaciers is where most accumulation occurs (inputs > outputs).
  ◦ The lower region is where most ablation occurs (inputs < outputs).
  ◦ The middle region is known as the line of equilibrium (inputs = outputs).

Physical factors affecting glaciated landscapes
- **Climate:** precipitation as snowfall is needed for accumulation which sustains and grows glaciers. In high altitude areas, such as mountainous regions, snowfall is often more frequent than in high latitude areas (north and south pole). High temperature and more rainfall contribute to ablation.
- **Geology:** hard, resistant rocks experience a slow rate of glacial erosion and so form steep sided valleys. Faults and joints in rock can be exploited by glacial erosion, and porous rock can also be vulnerable to water infiltration.
- **Latitude and altitude:** glaciers at lower latitudes receive more insolation, so they tend to occur at higher altitudes where temperatures drop, such as mountainous regions. At higher latitudes such as in Antarctica, glaciers often experience much drier, colder conditions so melting periods are shorter.
- **Relief and aspect:** gentle sloping landscapes allow for the accumulation of more snow and ice. Steeper slopes mean gravitational force is larger and glaciers can move downslope faster, causing faster erosion.

Types of glaciers and glacier movement
Formation of glaciers:
1. Glaciers begin to form when snow falls and remains frozen year round. Initial snowfall is referred to as névé. Snow that remains frozen for over a year is called a firn. Initially, the snow has a high air content and low density.
2. Over time, snow continues to fall and weighs down existing layers, making them increasingly compact and crystallised, forming high density ice that contains less air.
3. As the cycle of snowfall continues, density increases forcing out around 90% of air. Pure glacier ice has a density of $0.917 kg/m^3$. Over hundreds of years, glaciers form and their density gives them a deep blue colour due to low oxygen levels.

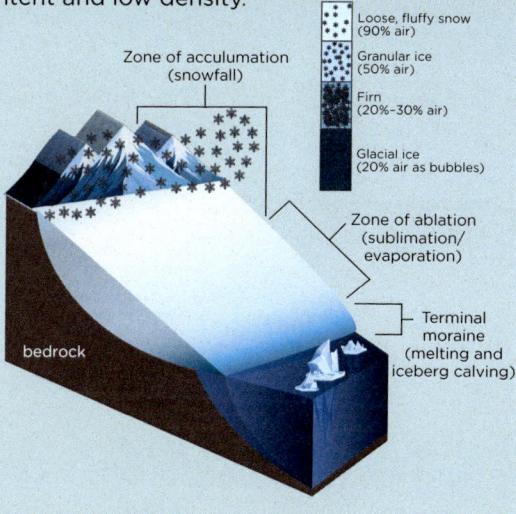

Types of glaciers:
- **Valley glaciers:** when dense ice forms within a steep sided V-shaped valley confined by mountain sides or pre-existing river valleys. They are narrow and vary in length, ranging from 3-4 km to over 7,000 km.
- **Ice sheets:** Antarctica and Greenland are the only two current ice sheets on Earth. They are large masses of ice that expand over $50,000 km^2$, though were much larger in previous ice ages.
- **Warm based glaciers:** typically found at mid latitude and high altitude regions with high snowfall and lots of basal movement due to ablation in summer. They have a large erosional impact due to lots of movement and activity.
- **Cold-based glaciers:** in high latitude very high altitude regions, these have sub-zero basal temperatures with very little meltwater or erosion as ice is frozen to bedrock.

Glacial movements:
- **Internal deformation:** main mechanism of movement for cold-based glaciers.
  ◦ If basal temperature is below 0, ice crystals deform and slowly slide past each other under lots of pressure when the glacier is on a slope
  ◦ When layers of glacial ice move at different rates, this is known as laminar flow.
- **Basal sliding:** main mechanism of movement for warm-based glaciers.
  ◦ If basal temperature is at/near the pressure melting point, there is a thin layer of meltwater at the base, reducing friction and allowing the ice to freely slide down.
  ◦ Ice at the upper part of the glacier is under more pressure, meaning it melts easier. When this happens, the meltwater flows down the edges of the glacier and freezes again once pressure is relieved in a process known as 'creep.'
  ◦ Deformation of the bed of sediment can occur where meltwater saturates it, allowing it to flow under the pressure of the glacier.

Glaciated landscapes

Development of glaciated landforms

Types of weathering affecting development of glaciated landforms		
Mechanical/physical	**Chemical**	**Biological**
• **Freeze thaw:** water fills small cracks in rock, freezes, and expands as ice which widens the crack over time causing it to split. • **Frost shattering:** continued melting and freezing of water in cracks of rocks causes them to disintegrate into small particles. • **Exfoliation:** when glaciers melt, pressure is removed from rock below, allowing it to expand which often causes it to break.	• **Carbonation:** rainwater absorbs atmospheric carbon dioxide forming weak carbonic acid that reacts with and dissolves certain rock. • **Oxidation:** oxygen in the atmosphere or water reacts with iron-rich rock and forms rust, weakening the rock and making it more prone to rockfall. • **Hydration:** water can chemically react with rock minerals, causing the surface to weaken and flake away.	• **Plant roots:** roots can grow into cracks of rock, forcing them open and weakening the rock. Burrowing animals can have a similar impact. • **Organic acids:** small plants like moss and lichen or algae can produce acids that react with rock and dissolve it (though this is limited in glacial landscapes where harsh climates mean little life exists).

- **Mass movement** is when gravitational force outweighs the upwards force of material, causing it to collapse. Examples include:
  - **Rockfalls:** when material dislodged by weathering along steep slopes it slides down and can be transported or accumulates as loose rock (scree).
  - **Landslides:** when meltwater saturates sediment, it becomes loose and can form a slurry of unstable rock that moves downslope. Slumps are increasingly likely when valleys are steep, or undercutting has occurred paired with wet conditions.
- **Nivation:** the pre-glacial formation of depressions in rock when weathering occurs under and around a patch of snow on rock due to a complex combination of freeze thawing and water washing away lose sediment.
- **Transportation:**
  - **Supraglacial** transportation is when debris is carried on the surface of glaciers.
  - **Subglacial** transportation carries debris at the base of the glacier.
  - **Englacial** transportation carries debris within its body.
  - Glaciers are supplied with sediment through many ways such as rockfalls, plucking, abrasion, or slurries.
- **Glacial deposition:**
  - **Till:** unsorted sediment deposited by ice.
  - **Outwash:** sorted sediment deposited by meltwater.

- **Glacial erosion:**
  - **Abrasion:** sediments and fragments of rock frozen in the base of the glacier scrape and erode the bedrock beneath it as it moves. This can leave behind smooth rock surfaces or striations depending on the size, shape and amount of debris.
  - **Plucking:** meltwater leaks into cracks within rocks and refreezes onto it. As the glacier moves, it pulls away the ice and any loose rock attached to it.

Erosional landforms	Corries	Hollows with steep back headwalls found in the upper parts of mountains or valleys. Formation often begins with nivation, As the depression grows, snow accumulates in it and over time a glacier forms. The glacier eventually develops its own circular movement that erodes further.
	Aretes	A pointed stretch of rock formed when two corries erode close to each other.
	Pyramidal peaks	When three or more corries erode towards each other forming a central rock peak.
	Troughs	When glaciers move through river valleys their powerful erosive action deepens and widens the valley.
	Roche moutonnée	A rock that is shaped by the movement of glaciers. Its upstream side is smooth with striations due to abrasion, whereas the downstream side is steep and rough due to glacial plucking under less pressure.
	Striations	Grooves marked into rock due to abrasion in the direction of glacier movement.
Depositional landforms	Terminal moraines	A ridge of till that follows the extent of the glacier's path, marking the point of the glacier's snout.
	Lateral moraines	Ridge of till deposited at the sides of valley glaciers where accumulation of sediment slides downwards as the glacier melts and retreats along the valley.
	Recessional moraines	Ridges of till deposited behind terminal moraine, occurring during a pause in glacial retreat.
	Erratics	Rocks that are comprised of varying geology types, or those foreign to the area it located due to being transported by the glacier over long distances before being deposited during ablation.
	Drumlins	Elongated hills of till that form parallel to the flow of ice.
	Till sheets	Large, flat stretches of till deposited when a wide area of glacier melts.

Glaciated landscapes

All specs except: CIE, Pearson IAL

Glacio-fluvial landforms and climate change

Glacio-fluvial landforms:
- **Kames:** mounds of stratefied debris that form when sediment fills crevasses. As the glacier retreats, meltwater loses energy quickly and deposits sediment at the snout or when a meltwater stream meets a still body of water.
  - Kame terraces are mounds of sediment that extend along the sides of valleys. This occurs when non-flowing channels form at the sides of glaciers due to the pressure between the ice and the valley walls. These collect sediment which is later deposited on the valley floor when the glacier has retreated.
- **Eskers:** long, winding ridges of sediment. Channels of meltwater carrying sediment flow beneath glaciers until they begin to melt which relieves pressure allowing the sediment to be deposited in the direction of retreat.
- **Outwash plains:** large, flat areas of deposited sediment in pro-glacial regions. Finer sediment is carried furthest by braided streams flowing away from the glacier's snout, depositing as it loses energy.

With increasing temperatures due to climate change, glacial retreat may begin to occur at a faster rate. This means more glacio-fluvial landforms may form and be more prominent. The last glacial period ended around 11,500 years ago and we are now in an interglacial period called the Holocene. Post-glacial periods occur when temperatures rise, increasing the volume of meltwater and developing various glacio-fluvial landforms.

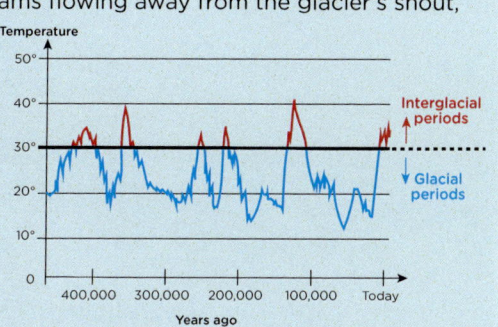

Periglacial landforms and climate change

Periglacial environments are at the margins of glaciers and ice sheets that experience freeze-thawing, particularly regions of permafrost where there are cycles of warmer and colder temperatures (e.g. Alaska, Siberia). Examples of periglacial landforms include:
- **Patterned ground:** repeated frost heave pushes rocks up and down the domes that form due to the swelling. This creates polygon shapes around each dome, creating patterns.
- **Pingos:** closed system pingos (often found in Canada) are found beneath lake beds. The water insulates the permafrost directly below it meaning it become talik (unfrozen ground). When the lake retreats, the talik freezes and forms a lens/core of ice that pushes upwards due to the hydrostatic pressure difference forming a hill. Open system pingos (often found in east Greenland) form when groundwater in talik under the permafrost collects beneath an area of weakness. Due to the pressure difference, the water is pushed upwards into the permafrost layer where it begins to freeze, forming an ice lens. As the core grows it pushes upwards and forms a hill.
- **Geomorphic processes in periglacial environments:**
  - **Freeze thaw weathering:** seasonal changes in temperature means that this process is an important process in these landscapes. The expansion and melting of ice in rock cracks means sediment is frequently broken down.
  - **Frost heave:** stones in the active layer have a low specific heat capacity. As water beneath them freezes and expands it pushes them upwards. Over time this action pushes stones to the surface.
- Increasing temperatures can impact these landforms. For example, melting permafrost and ice cores causes pingos to rupture and collapse inwards. For patterned ground, warmer temperatures may mean that freeze thawing is less extreme over time. A warmer environment also encourages vegetation colonisation so grasses and shrubs can grow.

Case study – inter-related glaciated landforms

	Laurentide Ice Sheet, North America
Physical factors in formation	• Vast, continental-scale ice coverage exerted immense pressure. • Thermal and flow regimes beneath the ice sheet, plus meltwater routing governed erosion and depositional patterns.
Inter-related landforms	• **Drumlins:** streamlined, teardrop-shaped hills oriented in direction of ice flow, formed of till – indicative of subglacial deformation. • **Eskers:** long, sinuous ridges of sorted sand and gravel deposited by subglacial meltwater channels. • **Kame-and-kettle topography:** mounds and depressions form as melting ice leaves behind sediment and buried ice blocks. • **Recessional and terminal moraines:** ridges of debris marking pauses in ice retreat or maximum advance.
Temporal changes	• **Within seconds:** sudden subglacial water surges can rapidly erode tunnel valleys or reshape meltwater channels (tunnel valleys may form over hundreds to thousands of years). • **Over seasons:** meltwater streams beneath the ice vary with seasonal thaw, influencing esker deposition and basal sliding. • **Over millennia:** gradual melting and retreat built the drumlin fields, esker networks, kame-and-kettle terrain, and moraines seen today.

Case study – human activity affecting periglacial landscapes

	Siberian permafrost degradation – Batagaika/Batagayskiy Crater, Russia
Human activity	• Triggered in the 1960s by forest clearance, human disturbance removed insulating vegetation, increasing ground warming and initiating permafrost thaw that formed the Batagaika Crater that has progressively expanded.
Impacts	• Thawing permafrost leads to ground subsidence and slope collapse, altering drainage and sediment flows. • The exposed cliff increases the surface area vulnerable to thaw, accelerating heat absorption and further melting in a positive feedback loop. • Retrogressive thaw slump: the crater is a rapidly expanding thermokarst feature characterised by horseshoe-shaped mass wasting and land collapse. • Thaw-induced instability causes continuous enlargement of the slump, reshaping periglacial terrain.
Landform changes	• Dramatically reshapes local topography and affects drainage patterns. • Destabilises surrounding slopes, threatening biodiversity and complicating any land use planning in the region

Dryland landscapes

Dryland landscapes as systems

Dryland landscapes are open systems, meaning energy can be transferred in and out:

Inputs	Precipitation (limited) and thermal energy from the sun
Processes	Weathering, erosion, and fluvial/aeolian transportation/deposition
Stores	Sediment and groundwater in aquifiers
Outputs	Evaporation/evapotranspiration, heat radiation into atmosphere, and surface runoff

- The Aridity Index (AI) is a numerical indicator used to measure the level of dryness of an environment. It calculates the ratio of precipitation (P) to potential evapotranspiration (PET). PET represents the maximum amount of water that could be evaporated if an abundance of water was available. The United Nations Environment Programme (UNEP) uses the equation:

$$AI = \frac{P}{PET}$$

where P = mean annual precipitation and PET = mean annual potential evapotranspiration.

Physical factors influencing dryland landscapes

- **Climate:** very low annual precipitation means more barren landscape, exposure to winds, and aeolian erosion. Long, dry seasons are broken by infrequent but intense and convective rainfall (caused by rising moist, warm air).
  ◦ Extreme arid regions = under 60 mm of mean annual precipitation.
  ◦ Arid regions = 60–250 mm of mean annual precipitation.
  ◦ Semi-arid regions = 250–500 mm of mean annual precipitation.
- **Geology:** impermeable rocks have high surface run off so rainwater cannot be drained, causing flash floods and erosive landforms like canyons. When rocks are very permeable (e.g. pumice, sandstone), water drains quickly below the surface leaving the top layer dry and ill-suited to vegetation (e.g. cold deserts in Iceland).
- **Latitude and altitude:** at latitudes of 20–30° in both hemispheres, the high pressure atmosphere inhibits cloud formation. This plus high solar radiation will form arid landscapes. Lower altitudes experience higher temperatures and drier climates which create more arid conditions. However, there are some dryland landscapes such as the Tibetan Plateau and Atacama Desert that are at high altitude.
- **Relief and aspect:** rain shadow deserts can form due to the orographic effect when humid air is pushed up one side of a mountain, cools, and produces precipitation. As the air descends the opposite side, it warms and dries out, encouraging a dryland landscape. If slopes are exposed to more sunlight or wind, then they may experience more erosion. Furthermore, steep slopes encourage faster surface runoff that causes increased rates of fluvial erosion.
- **Availability of sediment:** hard, rocky grounds (regs) or sandy grounds (ergs) have sediment supplied from weathering or fluvial and aeolian transportation.

Types of drylands

Polar drylands	Mid and low-altitude deserts	Semi-arid environments
• Located in Arctic regions • Experience very low temperatures and dry conditions • In short summer period, the top layer of ice melts and the active layer of permafrost thaws • When temperatures alternate from above and below 0 degrees, freeze-thaw weathering occurs • Example: Antarctica.	• Located in subtropical regions • High temperatures and very dry conditions with little annual precipitation • Mid latitude deserts have colder winters with a larger seasonal temperature range compared to low latitude • Example: Sahara Desert	• Located in several parts of the world including North America, Europe, Asia, and some parts of Africa • Have an aridity index between 0.20 and 0.50 • Experience more rainfall than more arid deserts but still prone to harsh droughts • Example: the Sahel region

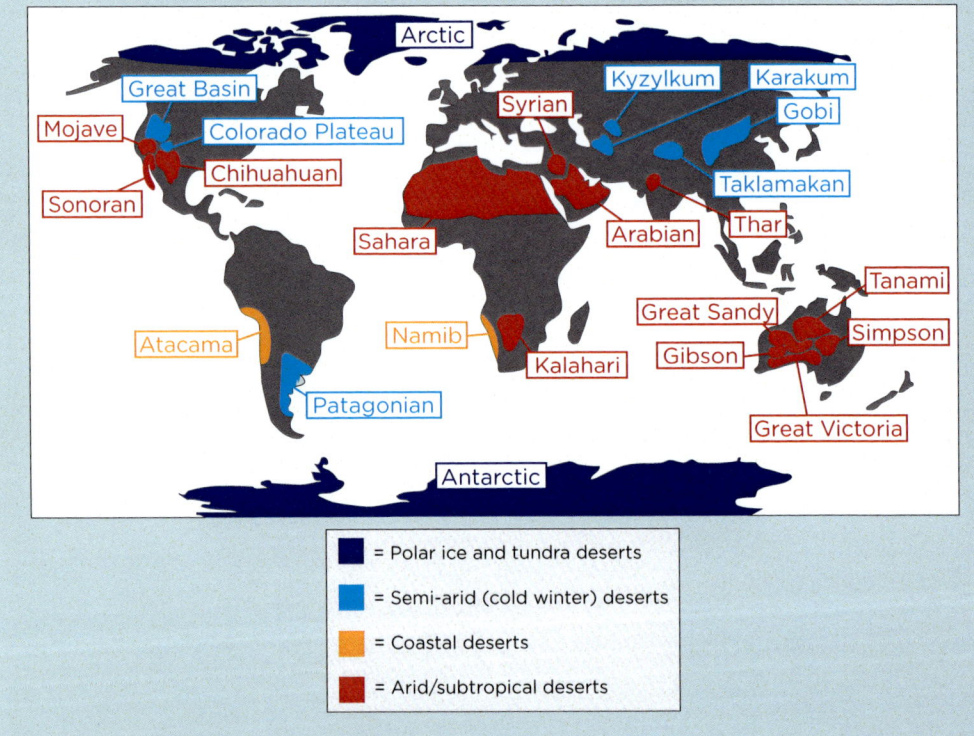

Dryland landscapes

Only: AQA, OCR, CIE

Development of dryland landscapes

Types of weathering affecting development of glaciated landforms		
Mechanical/physical	**Chemical**	**Biological**
• **Freeze thaw:** water fills small cracks in rock, freezes, expands as ice which widens the crack over time causing it to split. Occurs in colder months of mid-latitude deserts • **Salt weathering:** evaporation leaves salt crystals in pores of rock. Crystals expands and break the rock. • **Thermal expansion:** the cycle of contraction and expansion of rock due to temperature changes breaks down rock. • **Granular disintegration:** sediment of different shapes and sizes is weathered causing it to break down into grains.	• **Solution:** small particles dissolved in water can react with rock and break it down. • **Oxidation:** oxygen in the atmosphere or water reacts with iron-rich rock and forms rust, weakening the rock and making it more prone to rockfall. • **Hydration:** water can chemically react with rock minerals, causing the surface to weaken and flake away.	• **Plant roots:** dryland plants have extensive root systems that can grow into cracks of rock, forcing them open and weakening it. • **Organic acids:** some drylands have small plants like lichen or algae that can produce acids and CO_2 that reacts with rock and dissolve it.

- **Mass movement:** is when gravitational force outweighs the upwards force of material, causing it to collapse. Examples include:
  - **Rockfalls:** when weathering or erosion occurs at the base of a steep slope, the undercutting action causes rock above to collapse.
  - **Debris flows:** when flash floods occur during rare periods of heavy rainfall, water mixes with loose sediment and flows rapidly over the hard surface.
- **Fluvial (river) processes:** dryland landscapes experience minimal annual precipitation. However, when rainfall does occur it is usually heavy and intense.
  - Intense rainfall lands on extremely hard, dry rock meaning infiltration is limited so surface runoff is high.
  - Barren land means there are few barriers to prevent the flow of the water. As a result, fluvial erosion is powerful and can transport and deposit large volumes of sediment.
- **Aeolian (wind) processes:** strong winds are capable of eroding sandy landscapes in a process called deflation, where loose sand particles are picked up and moved by saltation.
  - These particles are often transported where they accumulate to form sand dunes once wind speed drops.
  - Sediment particles can also be pulled along the ground by wind in a process called 'creep'.

Erosional landforms	Wadis	Dry river valleys formed by powerful surface runoff and fluvial erosion during flash floods.
	Canyons	Deep, steep-sided, narrow river valleys formed by the downwards vertical erosion of hard rock caused by rivers.
	Pedestal rocks	Columns of rock that are narrow at the base, formed by aeolian erosion/saltation occurring lower to the ground.
	Ventifacts	Small rocks smoothed on one or more sides by aeolian abrasion.
	Desert pavements	Areas of ground comprised of flat, compacted stones formed by aeolian deflation where wind transports smaller sediment leaving behind larger rock fragments that interlock.
Depositional landforms	Barchans	Crescent shaped sand dunes with two points pointing downwind: one side of the crescent is steep, and one is gently sloping. These are formed when wind blows in one direction, depositing sand by saltation.
	Linear dunes	Long, narrow shaped dunes that form parallel to wind direction so are steep on both sides.
	Star dunes	Tall, pointed dunes that form when winds blow in multiple directions, depositing sand at and around a central point.
	Alluvial fans	When rare flash floods spread and their energy dissipates at the bottom of a steep gradient, they drop the large material they were transporting. This forms coned mounds of sediment at the bases of mountain fronts.
	Bajadas	Form when multiple alluvial fans join together.

Case study – inter-related dryland landscapes

	Great Basin Desert, USA (mid-latitude desert)	Sahara Desert (low-latitude/tropical desert)
Physical factors in formation	• Located in an interior plateau; aridity results from continental location and rain-shadow effects.	• Under the subtropical high-pressure belt; extreme aridity driven by descending dry air and negligible precipitation.
Inter-related landforms	• Wadis (ephemeral stream channels) channel infrequent but intense runoff; at canyon outlets, alluvial fans and bajadas form where energy drops.	• Aeolian landforms like dunes and deflation hollows coexist with wadis. Flash floods in these channels initiate erosional sculpting and deposit coarse material across desert pavements.
Temporal changes	• Within seconds: flash floods erode wadis and shift sediment. • Over millennia: repeated floods build up alluvial fans; pediments and inselbergs evolve slowly via weathering and erosion.	• Within seconds: sudden storms trigger flash floods that carve wadis and distribute sediment. • Over millennia: wind processes form sculptured rock features; dunes, hollows, and desert pavements slowly evolve.

Dryland landscapes

Only: AQA, OCR, CIE

Fluvial landforms resulting from pluvial periods
- 'Pluvial' refers to periods of time where the climate was wetter in an area that is now a dryland.
- Many current dryland regions once experienced more humid and wet weather, allowing for permanent rivers, bodies of water, wildlife, and vegetation to be sustained.
- **Landforms influenced by pluvial periods:**
  - Wadis and canyons are formed by fluvial erosion which would have been much more prominent in pluvial periods when streams and rivers were permanent.
  - Water is essential for the formation of alluvial fans and bajadas. During pluvial periods, the rate of their development was much faster due to increased rates of fluvial erosion and deposition.
  - Inselbergs are steep sided mountains of hard rock, isolated in their surroundings. They form when erosional processes (such as those heightened in pluvial periods) break down surrounding soft rock, leaving behind the resistant rock as inselbergs.
  - Playa basins are also an example of landforms influenced by pluvial periods. They are dry lake beds that were once permanent water bodies.
- **Present and future modifications to pluvial landforms:**
  - Erosion still occurs, but mainly through aeolian processes rather than fluvial processes. Dryland conditions make deflation and abrasion more dominant, especially due to the lack of vegetation, availability of dry, loose sediment, and strong winds.
  - Fluvial erosion is still present with occasional flash flooding meaning landforms like canyons and wadis can develop but at a slower rate.
  - In the future, climate change may mean that temperatures in arid drylands increases, and rainfall becomes more infrequent yet more intense so fluvial erosion may increase.

Periglacial landforms resulting from colder periods
- **Periglacial:** environments found at the margins of glaciers and ice sheets that experience freeze-thawing, particularly regions of permafrost where there are cycles of warmer and colder temperatures.
- **Geomorphic processes in periglacial environments:**
  - **Freeze thaw weathering:** seasonal changes in temperature means that this process is an important process in these landscapes. The expansion and melting of ice in rock cracks means sediment is frequently broken down.
  - **Frost heave:** stones in the active layer have a low specific heat capacity. As water beneath them freezes and expands it pushes them upwards. Over time this action pushes stones to the surface.
- These processes helped to form landforms in drylands that are now relict:
  - Frost shattering occurs when freeze-thaw weathering breaks rocks apart, leaving behind blockfields and scree.
  - Nivation hollows can also be seen. These are hollows in rock when weathering occurs under and around a patch of snow on rock due to a complex combination of freeze thawing and water washing away lose sediment.
  - Solifluction happens when thawed saturated soil of the top layer slides downslope over permafrost, leaving behind unsorted mounds of debris.
- **Present and future modification to periglacial landforms:**
  - After the glacial period, periglacial landforms become relict.
  - Fluvial erosion still occurs during flash floods which alters these landforms. Similarly, aeolian erosion is dominant in the dry landscapes where strong winds easily carry fine sediments, slowing wearing down the relict landforms.
  - Future climate change may cause higher intensity rainfall that increases the power of fluvial erosion during flash floods, causing further wearing down of pre-existing landforms.

Case study – water supply issues in dryland landscapes

	Neckartal Dam and Fish River Oasis, Namibia
Water supply issues	• The Neckartal Dam, built in 2019, provides reliable water storage in a dryland region where communities depend on sporadic floodwater.
Impacts	• The dam impounds around 80 % of the desert oasis basin runoff, significantly reducing downstream water availability. • Results include channel narrowing (~15%) and roughly a 20% decrease in sediment yield downstream, altering the natural sediment transport regime.
Landform changes	• Reduced flows mean that smaller, more frequent floods no longer occur; only extremely rare large floods can overcome the dam to transport sediment and maintain downstream pool-bar morphology. • As a result, depositional features are being eroded or not replenished, weakening the development of distributary channels and alluvial fans. • The oasis ecosystem is shifting: chronic low flows favour invasive species and disrupt the fragile desert landscape. • Sediment accumulation upstream and reduced downstream replenishment reshape drainage patterns and diminish the resilience of flood-dependent landforms.

Water and carbon cycles

Importance of water and carbon systems for life on Earth

The carbon and water cycles are examples of natural systems. Systems are comprised of inputs, stores, processes, and outputs. Systems can be:
- Open (energy can be transferred in and out of them)
- Closed (no energy can be transferred in or out)

Water and carbon cycles on a global scale are closed as there is no significant input or output of matter or energy to/from Earth. However, they can be open when considered at a local scale, such as a river basin or forest.

Water cycle

- **Global distribution:**
  - 97% in oceans
  - 3% freshwater of which 30% is groundwater, 68% is in the cryosphere.

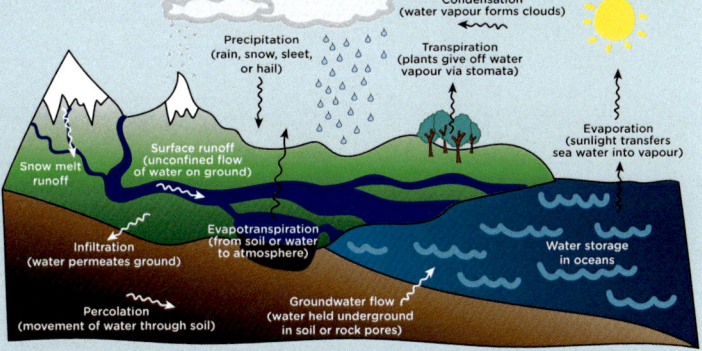

- **Inputs and outputs:**
  - **Precipitation:** water in the form of rain, sleet, hail or snow enters through drainage basins. This is the primary input to water systems. It is also an output when evaporation occurs back into the atmosphere.
  - **Ablation:** the loss of water from the cryosphere via melting or sublimation, returning water back into rivers and oceans through drainage basins.
  - **Evapotranspiration:** a major output where water is released into the atmosphere when it is evaporated and condensed to be returned via precipitation.
- **Processes:**
  - **Evaporation:** water is heated and converted into water vapour in the atmosphere
  - **Transpiration:** the release of water as vapour from plants' stomata.
  - **Condensation:** when water vapour cools and forms liquid droplets suspended in the atmosphere. This also explains the formation of clouds.
  - **Precipitation:** water released from clouds.
  - **Interception:** when precipitation is temporarily interrupted by surfaces such as plant leaves or branches before it eventually falls to the ground or evaporates.
  - **Ablation:** the process of cryosphere stores melting, evaporation or sublimating.
  - **Runoff:** water moves over land towards larger bodies of water like oceans or rivers when the ground has become fully saturated and cannot hold excess water.
  - **Catchment hydrology:** begins with infiltration where water drains from the surface into the soil. Then water percolates down through soil and rock into the groundwater layer. Throughflow then takes place along the soil before it reaches groundwater and emerges at water sources and springs.

Carbon cycle

- **Global distribution:**
  - Lithosphere: 99.985%
  - Hydrosphere: 0.0076%
  - Pedosphere: 0.0031%
  - Cryosphere: 0.0018%
  - Atmosphere: 0.0015%
  - Biosphere: 0.0012%

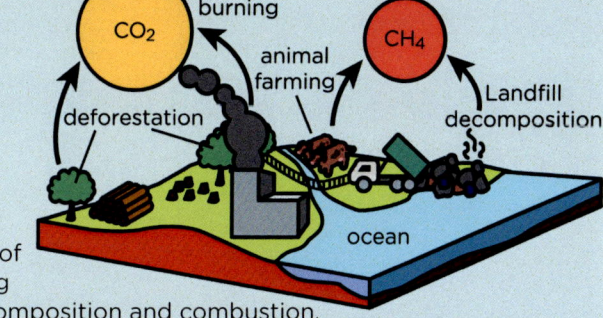

- **Fast carbon cycle:** involves the quick processes and movement of carbon between stores, including photosynthesis, respiration, decomposition and combustion.
- **Slow carbon cycle:** involves the movement of carbon over long periods of time (thousands or millions of years), including weathering or formation of fossil fuels.
- **Inputs and outputs:**
  - **Precipitation:** carbon reacts with water in the atmosphere forming weak carbonic acid, chemically weathering rocks and releasing carbon.
  - **Photosynthesis:** plants remove CO_2 from the atmosphere and release oxygen.
  - **Decomposition:** decomposers such as bacteria and fungi in the environment break down dead organic matter into carbon compounds which are released into soil. Carbon is also released into the atmosphere due to the respiration of decomposers.
  - **Weathering:** weak carbonic acid reacts and breaks down rick, releasing carbon into the atmosphere.
  - **Respiration:** respiring organisms use glucose and oxygen to release carbon dioxide into the atmosphere as one of the products.
  - **Combustion:** burning of stored carbon releases it into the atmosphere.
- **Processes:**
  - **Photosynthesis:** the process by which plants absorb carbon dioxide from the atmosphere and convert it into glucose and oxygen using light energy and water.
  - **Respiration:** the process by which organisms break down glucose to release energy, releasing CO_2 and water as byproducts.
  - **Decomposition:** the breakdown of dead organic matter by bacteria and fungi, releasing CO_2 into the soil and atmosphere whilst maintaining nutrient cycles.
  - **Combustion:** burning carbon storing organic material, releasing carbon dioxide into the atmosphere. This can be naturally such as through wildfires or can be human induced for example: burning fossil fuels or slash-burn methods of clearing forest.
  - **Natural sequestration:** carbon sequestration refers to the capturing and long-term storage of CO_2 from the atmosphere into stores such as oceans, soil and forests. CO_2 can be absorbed by phytoplankton in oceans, stores in vegetation through photosynthesis or stored in sediments after millions of years of build-up of dead organic matter.

Water and carbon cycles

Case study – water and carbon cycles in tropical rainforests and Arctic tundra

	The Amazon Rainforest	Alaskan Arctic Tundra
Water cycle	• Mean annual precipitation is >2000 mm. • High rates of evapotranspiration and absolute humidity • Intense rainfall means soils are saturated and well drained with lots of water stored as groundwater or in aquifers. • High interception from dense vegetation.	• Low mean annual precipitation between 150–250 mm. • Low temperatures mean limited evapotranspiration and low absolute humidity. • Permafrost layer limits infiltration so drainage is poor.
Factors affecting water cycle	• Temperature: high temperatures mean high evapotranspiration, and convection occurs in a feedback loop, increasing precipitation. • Geology: rocks in the Amazon are mostly impermeable and form a crystalline layer in the basin. This limits the amount of infiltration which coincides with an increase in runoff. • Relief: it is a lowland region, meaning overland flow of water occurs along the gently sloping land into rivers and stored in floodplains.	• Temperature: sub-zero temperatures mean most water is frozen and stored as ice therefore evapotranspiration and infiltration is low. In the short summer season the top layer melts, ground becomes waterlogged and a network of lakes and ponds form. • Rock permeability: impermeable bedrock and permafrost limits groundwater movement and throughflow. • Relief: surface runoff is slow due to the mostly flat surface.
Human impact on the water cycle	• Deforestation: around 20% of the Amazon rainforest has been cleared for logging or agriculture, dramatically reducing interception and increasing surface runoff and flash flood risk. • Cattle ranching and overgrazing can cause erosion of soil, compacting it into the ground meaning more surface runoff.	• Heat released from oil and gas industries melt permafrost faster. • The addition of roads and buildings disturbs the limited natural drainage processes meaning any infiltration is further reduced. • Thawing period of the active layer in warmer periods grows, so there is more meltwater and inundation, causing excess surface runoff and floods.
Carbon cycle	• The Amazon stores approximately 123 billion tonnes of carbon in its biomass, soil, and organic matter. • High rates of photosynthesis and carbon fixation. • Warm, humid conditions mean decomposition occurs rapidly. • High carbon sequestration (absorbing lots of atmospheric carbon).	• Permafrost is a huge carbon sink storing 1,600 billion metric tonnes of carbon. • Decomposition rates are low due to low temperatures. • Biomass stored in vegetation is low due to harsh climates however plants grow during the warmer periods in summer when the active layer thaws. • Low net primary productivity.
Factors affecting carbon cycle	• Temperature: high temperature speeds up decomposition and photosynthesis. • Vegetation: densely packed flora are large carbon stores, forming carbon-rich organic matter when they decompose.	• Temperature: cold temperatures slow down decomposition. In summer months, photosynthesis occurs, increasing uptake of carbon. • Rock permeability: limited carbon source from rocks due to their impermeability and low porosity
Human impact on carbon cycle	• Deforestation releases carbon stored in biomass and reduces the availability of vegetation to photosynthesise and absorb carbon from the atmosphere in biomass, so carbon sequestration falls. • Slash and burn methods of clearing forest are very damaging, releasing CO_2 which further damages the environment.	• Permafrost melting due to heat from human activity means vast stores of carbon are released into the atmosphere. • Clearance of vegetation reduces photosynthesis and carbon sequestration.
Management strategies	• Afforestation/reforestation programmes increases interception and evapotranspiration by restoring carbon sinks. • Areas of the rainforest are now classified as national parks to protect them from illegal logging and exploitation. • REDD+ is a UN program that has established financial incentives for indigenous groups to protect the rainforest. • Improving agricultural techniques such as reducing monocultures and overcultivation to restore soil fertility and diversity.	• Using pipelines that are elevated above ground reduces disturbance to the environment. • Insulating pipelines and infrastructure reduces the thermal energy released. This slows the melting of permafrost, protecting carbon stores. • Using fewer drilling sites reduces the impact of human activity to a limited number of sites.

Water and carbon cycles

Human factors affecting water and carbon processes and stores

The global carbon and water cycles are naturally in a state of **dynamic equilibrium**, where in the long term there is balance between all inputs, stores and outputs of each system. This is maintained by negative feedback loops that help to regulate the balance, whereas positive feedback loops occur when an initial change is amplified and continues to change.

Land use changes that can alter the water and carbon cycles		
Urbanisation	Farming	Forestry
• Impermeable surfaces like concreate and tarmac reduces infiltration and percolation of water into soil, increasing surface runoff. • Urban areas reduce the amount of vegetation cover. This reduces interception of precipitation and lowers the amount of carbon that can be stored via photosynthesis. • Artificial drainage systems can inundate natural rivers and streams.	• Repeated ploughing and cultivation expose soil carbon to oxidation and reduces soil moisture. • Irrigation systems add water to the environment, increasing infiltration. • Farming livestock releases lots of methane into the atmosphere. • Farming practices often require deforestation, reducing natural carbon storage, interception, and evapotranspiration.	• Afforestation enhances carbon sequestration by adding available carbon stores. • More trees and vegetation mean levels of evapotranspiration and interception, reducing runoff.

- Water extraction by humans can have effects of the water cycle.
  ○ **Surface extraction** is when water is removed from stores such as lakes and reservoirs to meet domestic and industrial needs such as for agriculture, public water supply or for manufacturing processes. **Sub-surface extraction** is when water is removed from aquifers or artesian basins (groundwater that is under artesian pressure).
  ○ The **over-extraction of groundwater** has damaging impacts, such as falling in water tables. For example, the River Kennet experienced over extraction, meaning the volume of water extracted was more than the volume of water being naturally replaced. Over extraction may cause vegetation and wetlands to dry up which has damaging effects on wildlife.
- **Fossil fuel combustion** refers to the burning of coal, oil or gas. This leads to the release of large volumes of carbon dioxide into the atmosphere, enhancing the greenhouse effect and can cause long term damage to the global carbon cycle. Yearly CO_2 emissions due to the burning of these fossil fuels totals to around 34 billion tonnes per year.
  ○ Carbon Capture and Storage (CCS): works by capturing CO_2 at the source, then transporting it to be stored deep underground so it does not enter the atmosphere. It may be successful but requires large amounts of energy and is currently quite expensive.

Examples of carbon cycle feedback loops:
- **Positive feedback:** increased greenhouse gas emissions leads to increasing global temperature. This causes permafrost and ice in arctic regions to melt. This releases more carbon into the atmosphere, further increasing temperatures and escalating the process.
- **Negative feedback:** higher levels of carbon in the atmosphere mean more carbon is available for photosynthesis. This means more carbon can then be stored long term.

Examples of water cycle feedback loops:
- **Positive feedback:** warming climate leads to increased rates of evaporation. This produces more water vapour which is a greenhouse gas. This then causes further warming due to enhanced greenhouse gas effect.
- **Negative feedback:** increased evaporation due to warmer climates may also have a cooling effect. More water vapour means more cloud formation which helps to reflect solar radiation.

Pathways and processes controlling water and carbon cycles

		Water cycle	Carbon cycle
Short-term changes	Diurnal (daily)	• Evaporation rates from plants are higher during the day when more solar radiation is available. • Transpiration from plants reduce at night when stomata close. • Precipitation is more common during the daytime.	• Photosynthesis only occurs during the day when light energy from the sun is available. • At night, photosynthesis stops, and carbon dioxide is released into the atmosphere.
	Seasonal	• Summer months with higher temperatures mean more evaporation and transpiration. • Winter months means more water can be stored as ice. • Precipitation is also lowest during summer months in the UK.	• More photosynthesis occurs during summer months where more carbon dioxide is absorbed from the atmosphere into the biosphere. • In winter months, leaf fall and the decomposition of this organic matter means the carbon is released back into the atmosphere.
Long-term changes		• During glacial periods, more water is stored in the cryosphere. • This means sea level is lower, and rates of evaporation and precipitation are reduced.	• During glacial periods, levels of atmospheric carbon is lower in comparison to interglacial periods. • Permafrost and cryosphere act as large, long-term store for carbon. • Reduction in vegetation in glacial periods means less carbon is stored in the biosphere.

- To understand the impact of human activity on the climate, predict future changes and form mitigation strategies; monitoring and research techniques are needed. These may include:
  ○ **Ice cores:** deep tubes of ice show the historic pattern of carbon presence in the atmosphere.
  ○ **Satellite imagery:** satellites can be used to display patterns of indicators such as global vegetation cover or ice mass. The data can then be used to map future trends and changes to the carbon and water cycles.
  ○ **Sea surface temperature:** the temperature of the upper few millimetres of ocean indicates patterns of global warming and carbon absorption.

Water and carbon cycles

Interdependence of water and carbon cycles

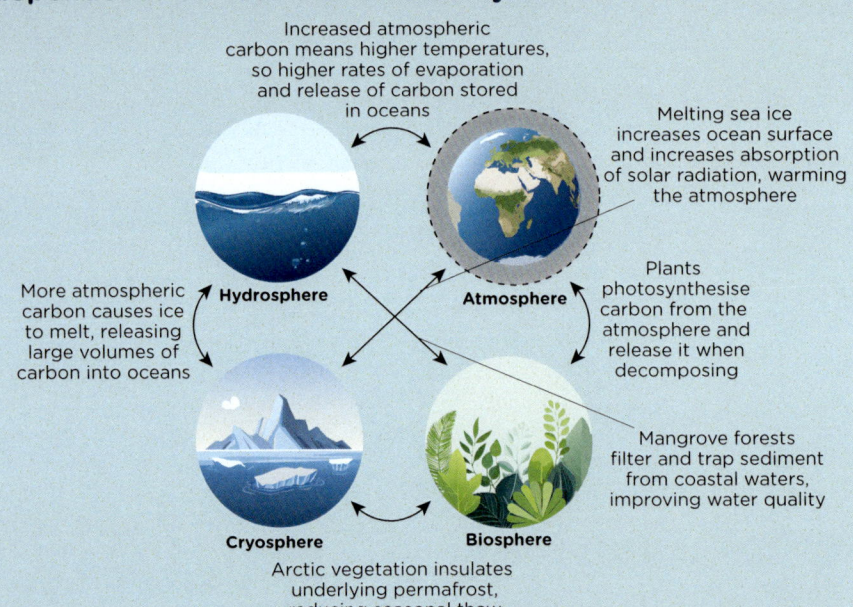

Increased atmospheric carbon means higher temperatures, so higher rates of evaporation and release of carbon stored in oceans

Melting sea ice increases ocean surface and increases absorption of solar radiation, warming the atmosphere

More atmospheric carbon causes ice to melt, releasing large volumes of carbon into oceans

Plants photosynthesise carbon from the atmosphere and release it when decomposing

Mangrove forests filter and trap sediment from coastal waters, improving water quality

Arctic vegetation insulates underlying permafrost, reducing seasonal thaw and slowing the release of stored carbon and meltwater

- **The impact of human activities on the availability of carbon and water stores:**
  - **Population increase and rising demand:** as the demand for water for public and industrial use increases, more water is extracted from sources to meet demands. This has damaging impacts on groundwater levels and the water table.
  - **Deforestation:** removal of vegetation means precipitation is no longer intercepted. Surface runoff increases whilst simultaneously decreasing infiltration rates. This also causes soil erosion and limits groundwater recharge, meaning many landscapes dry out. Removing vegetation also limits the amount of carbon that can be stored in biomass.
  - **Fossil fuels:** combustion of fossil fuels adds tonnes of carbon the atmosphere, where it enhances the greenhouse effect.
- **Impact of long-term climate change on the cycles:**
  - **Water cycle:** as temperatures increase, as does evaporation and the amount of water vapour in the atmosphere which accelerates warming further. This warming causes water stored in the cryosphere to melt which rises sea levels. More evaporation also leads to more precipitation and extreme weather events.
  - **Carbon cycle:** global warming means less carbon dioxide is absorbed by oceans and the melting of permafrost releases carbon into the atmosphere. Warmer temperatures also mean that decomposition occurs faster, so more carbon is released into the biosphere or atmosphere.

Global implications of water and carbon management

Global management strategies to protect the global carbon cycle	
Strategy	Description
Afforestation	Planting trees absorbs carbon dioxide from the atmosphere through photosynthesis, enhancing the terrestrial carbon store. One example of this is China's Great Green Wall to increase carbon sequestration and reduce desertification.
Wetland restoration	Wetland landscapes like peatbogs and marshes can store large amounts of carbon, however human activity has damaged them. Restoration projects around the world have started to recover wetlands using methods such as controlled floods or diverting water channels.
Improving agricultural practices	Limiting tillage and overcultivation means the amount of carbon that can be stored in soil is maintained. Improving animal feed can reduce the amount of methane produced by livestock management. Furthermore, preventing deforestation for agriculture will protect forest carbon storage.
Reducing emissions	Cap and Trade scheme was introduced as an incentive to reduce carbon emissions of businesses by allowing trade of credits earned for emitting less carbon or receiving penalties for emitting too much.

Global management strategies to protect the global water cycle	
Strategy	Description
Improving forestry techniques	The REDD+ (Reducing Emissions from Deforestation Degradation) programme is an initiative led by the UN which supports countries in restoring their forests.
Water allocations	When water is in limited supply, it must be divided and rationed between those who need it: such as businesses, agriculture and the public. To reduce wastage of water, solutions such as drip irrigation and recycling can be used.
Drainage basin planning	This involves management plans to protect drainage basins by balancing the water demands of industries, the public and ecosystems. In the UK, river basin management plans set targets for abstraction, runoff, and habitat protection.

Exploring oceans

Oceans as a distinctive feature of the Earth

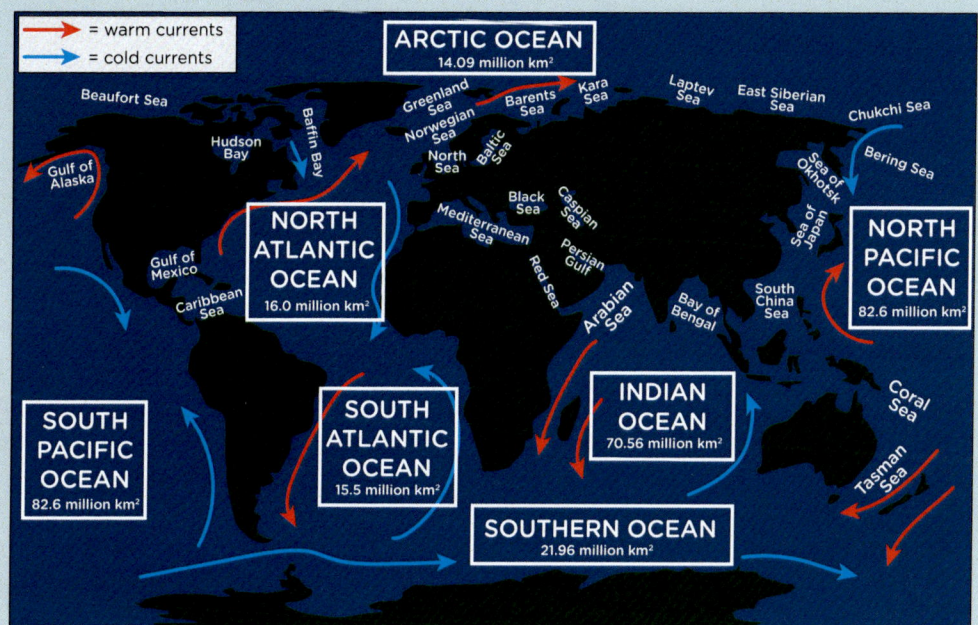

- Ocean temperature is warmest at the equator, then begins to decrease towards the tropics, mid latitudes and finally the polar regions where it is coldest (due to higher solar radiation at the equator). Temperature also decreases with depth.
- Salinity refers to the concentration of dissolved salts in the water. The halocline refers to the change in salinity with depth.
- The North Atlantic circulation involves a complex system of currents. Heat energy is transported along the Gulf stream near Mexico, along the coast of North America and past West Europe towards the Arctic. Cold water flows down from this region towards Canada and the USA.

Ocean basin relief:
- At the edges of continents, continental shelf extends out into the ocean and are gently sloping with a depth of around 200 m.
- This then extends into a narrow continental slope, steeper than shelves and often cut by canyons.
- Abyssal plains are flat deep areas of the ocean. Along these plains, ridges form where divergent plate boundaries meet. One example of this is the Mid-Atlantic ridge where magma rises, and volcanic activity occurs.
- Ocean trenches are very deep depressions in the ocean basin. For example, the Mariana trench: the deepest point of the ocean.
- Guyots are submerged mountains with flat tops, often formed when an extinct volcano is eroded.

Factors influencing ocean biodiversity
- **Changes in light intensity:** light can only penetrate to a certain depth in the ocean. Surface water receives most light, meaning photosynthesis can occur. Beneath the surface, light intensity decreases exponentially and at depths of over 1,000 metres, no light penetrates at all. This is called the aphotic zone.
- **Changes in temperature:** ocean temperature decreases with depth and latitude. This is linked to light intensity as temperature is mainly linked to heat transferred from light emitted by the sun.
- **Changes in nutrient supply:** nutrient levels increase with depth. Upwelling zones of water bring cold, nutrient-rich water to the surface. Decomposition of organisms also provides the ocean with nutrients as dead organic matter sinks and is recycled.

Inter tidal water	Deep water
• Nutrient input mainly comes from waves and tides. • Temperatures fluctuate seasonally • Biodiversity is high • Food chains are short and simple • Example: salt marshes	• Nutrient input is from ice and sinking organic matter • Cold temperatures • Biodiversity is moderately low • Food chains are long and complex • Example: Antarctic marine life

Use of ocean energy and mineral resources
- **Non-renewable** energy resources from the ocean include oil and gas, found at continental shelves and extracted via drilling rigs.
  - Advantages: these resources are vital for many industrial economies, and the building and operating of rigs provides lots of employment opportunities.
  - Disadvantages: large risk of oil spills which have devastating effects on the ecosystem and organisms. They also release high carbon emissions and disturb marine life and habitats.
- **Renewable** energy resources can also be produced from the ocean. Wave energy can be generated water columns and from the motion of the water. Tidal energy can also be generated from the rise and fall of water level.
  - Advantages: resources are renewable and not finite like oil and gas. They produce far less carbon emissions and also provide employment opportunities.
  - Disadvantages: initial costs are high, and facilities can be expensive to maintain. The sites may still disturb coastal ecosystems and marine life.
- **Seabed minerals:** ferrous seabed minerals refer to iron containing metals, non-ferrous minerals do not contain iron. These minerals are an opportunity for underwater mining, extracting these minerals means they can be used in technological manufacturing and other processes. The process involves mining for nodules of metals like manganese and other rare metals which can be used in solar panels, electric car batteries and more. Despite this, there are issues with deep sea mining. There is a lot that is unknown about deep ocean ecosystems, so mining could cause irreversible damage. Waste materials may also pollute the marine environment.

Exploring oceans

Only: OCR, WJEC, Eduqas

Governing the oceans and resource management
Who owns the oceans is a contested topic.
- **Global commons**: areas and resources that are not controlled by a single country or region, so are accessible to everyone (e.g. oceans, atmosphere, and outer space).
- **Tragedy of the commons:** Garrett Hardin argued that tragedy of the commons occurs when resources are exploited by individuals or states out of their own interest. For example, oceans have been openly accessible to people to fish in, however this has led to the overfishing of certain areas and damage to species.
- **Zoning of oceans:**
  - The water that extends 0-12 nautical miles (nm) from land is territorial water, owned and controlled by countries. Within this, from 3-12 nm, the water is owned by the country, but foreign vessels have right to innocent passage (known as the contiguous zone).
  - From 0-200 nm, the water is known as the Exclusive Economic Zone (EEZ) where countries have rights to explore and use the resources found there.
  - Beyond 200 nm is known as the high seas. The water is not controlled by any sovereignty and is accessible to all.
  - Where zones overlap, conflict may occur.
- **The United Nations Convention on the Law of the Sea (UNCLOS)** are an international organisation that set regulations and frameworks for the governance of oceans. This includes outlining the rights each country has to the seas and how they should be treated.
- **International Seabed Authority (ISA):** established in 1982 to monitor the activity and exploitation of resources found in the seabed. They are responsible for protecting the oceans from the effects of harmful human activity
- **Marine reserves:** areas of ocean where human activity and exploitation is prohibited or highly controlled to protect ecosystems. Currently only 8% of Earth's ocean is a Marine Protected Area (MPA).

Case study - dangers of offshore oil production

	Deepwater Horizon Oil Spill, Gulf of Mexico (2010)
Causes	• Well blowout during drilling: a failure in the Macondo Prospect well on April 20, 2010, led to an uncontrolled release of oil and gas after high-pressure hydrocarbons escaped into the wellbore. • Multiple safety and equipment failures: contributing factors included defective cement sealing, misinterpretation of pressure test data, and the malfunction of the blowout preventer.
Impacts on marine ecosystems	• ~4.9 million barrels of crude oil released over 87 days. • Oil slick covered ~149,000 km² of ocean surface. • Severe contamination of coastal wetlands, beaches, and estuaries. • Mass mortality of marine life and long-term impacts on benthic communities due to oil deposition on seabed.
Impacts on human activities	• Collapse of commercial and recreational fishing in affected areas due to contamination and fishing bans. • Loss of tourism revenue from beach closures and publicity. • Health issues among clean-up workers from chemical exposure. • Billions of dollars in economic losses for Gulf Coast communities.
Management strategies	• Immediate containment efforts: capping wellhead, controlled burns, skimming oil, and applying dispersants. • Shoreline clean-up using manual removal, high-pressure washing, and bioremediation. • BP and USA government established a $20 billion compensation fund for affected businesses and individuals. • Long-term restoration: habitat rehabilitation, monitoring of fisheries, and stricter offshore drilling regulations.

Pollutants affecting ocean systems
- **Pollution from combustion of fossil fuels:** ships and industry vessels release large amounts of pollutants into the water and air which can be absorbed by oceans.
- **Pollution from domestic and industrial processes:** plastics can end up in the ocean for a multitude of reasons. Littering by tourists and workers in the sea, waste from industry and lost fishing gear are some examples. Many countries also discharge waste and sewage into seas and oceans, which can have damaging environmental effects. Despite this, many advanced countries are finding alternative ways of disposing this waste.
  - Nuclear waste can end up in oceans. Leaks from nuclear power plants or nuclear accidents (such as at Fukushima) can enter ecosystems. These leaks are very hard to control and manage, having long-lasting effects on marine life including pollution of habitats and genetic mutations.
- **Marine debris:** such as plastics, fishing gear, and metals are examples of waste that end up in the ocean as a result of human activities. Debris enters the ocean from rivers, purposeful dumping or losses of material and products after storms. Surface currents move this debris across oceans and can provide useful findings as to how currents work worldwide. Despite this, the consequences of pollution are very damaging.
  - Plastics are not biodegradable – they break down into **microplastics** that infiltrate into marine food chains and even human drinking water systems.
  - For example, the **Great Pacific Garbage Patch** in the North Pacific Gyre (between Hawaii and Alaska) is the largest accumulation of plastic waste in the ocean. This debris is transported by currents and trapped in the gyre's convergence zone, leading to the entanglement and death of marine life, bioaccumulation of toxic chemicals, and habitat disruption.

Exploring oceans

Only: OCR, WJEC, Eduqas

Climate change affecting oceans
- **Impacts of ocean acidification:** the ocean absorbs large amount of carbon from the atmosphere, storing approximately 30% of anthropogenic emissions. As carbon dioxide reacts with water, it causes its pH to lower, meaning acidity increases.
  - Higher acidity reduces the availability of calcium carbonate, a crucial molecule needed for shellfish and corals to form their shells and skeletons.
  - This has knock on effects on the nutrient cycle as less carbon sinks to the seafloor during decomposition to replenish carbon stores in the seabed.
  - The acidity also impacts the reproduction and development stages of fish, impacting food security, the fishing industry, and marine life.
- **The impact of rising temperature on coral ecosystems:** corals are extremely vulnerable to changes in environmental conditions. When temperature, salinity, and light conditions change, corals expel algae from their surface, causing coral bleaching. UNEP estimate a 14% loss in coral reef occurred between 2009 and 2018.
- **The impact on sea levels:** as the climate becomes warmer, ice sheets and other stores in the cryosphere begin to melt. This rises relative sea level.
- **The impact on high latitude oceans:** high latitude oceans (Arctic, Southern) are rapidly warming. The extent of ice coverage decreased by an average of 12.1% each decade from 1979 to 2024, with ice retreating earlier in summer and reforming later in winter. As ice coverage depletes, albedo also decreases. Ice can reflect most of the sun's radiation back into space, whereas water absorbs most of this radiation and heat energy so as ice continues to melt, it will reach a tipping point where albedo keeps decreasing and warming will continue in a positive feedback loop.

Case study – threats to island communities

	Pacific Ocean threats to Kiribati
Threats	• Sea-level rise (projected 0.4–1.0 m by 2100) threatens to submerge low-lying atolls (average elevation < 2 m). • Saltwater intrusion contaminates freshwater lenses, reducing potable water supply and damaging crops. • Coastal erosion intensified by storm surges and loss of protective coral reefs due to ocean acidification. • Increased cyclone intensity linked to climate change.
Impacts	• Loss of homes and agricultural land; displacement of residents to urban South Tarawa, causing overcrowding. • Declining food security from reduced taro, fruit, and fish yields. • Rising health risks from waterborne diseases.
Short-term adaptations	• Building sea walls and coastal revetments • Rainwater harvesting and desalination to secure drinking water • Community mangrove planting to stabilise shorelines
Long-term adaptations	• Government's 'Migration with Dignity' policy - agreements with New Zealand and Fiji for gradual relocation • Promotion of climate-resilient crops and aquaculture

Globalisation of oceans
- **Global shipping patterns:**
  - Two main examples of routes include the Trans-Atlantic route which connects Europe to west of the USA and the Trans-Pacific route which connects Asia to North America.
  - Pinch points such as the Suez Canal and Panama Canal can create blockages and majorly disrupt the movement of cargo.
  - Since globalisation and the rise in containerisation, the number and size of cargo ships has increased, putting pressure on these routes and pinch points.
  - An example of this was in 2021 when the blockage of the Suez Canal caused widespread chaos and disruption to supply chains.
- **International conflicts:** oceans have long been an area of conflict for countries willing to access resources, develop military protection or improve trade security. Many historical battles have occurred at sea.
  - One example of a country that has recently exerted naval influence is the USA, which has developed multiple naval bases in over 20 countries, including multiple in Japan, Korea, and Singapore. These bases allow the USA to exert geopolitical power globally and maintain control over problems relating to trade or security threats. Bases in Asia are extremely important amongst growing tensions in the South China Sea.
  - The South China Sea dispute is one example of marine tension. Conflict surrounding the ownership of seas between China, Vietnam, and the Philippines has led to a growth in military presence in the region.
- **Modern piracy**: this involves the armed robbery or hijacking of vessels at sea or within harbours. Piracy incidences have been increasing since the rise in global shipping routes.
  - Examples of areas that experience high numbers of piracy incidences include: the west coast of Africa (particularly the Gulf of Guinea), the Gulf of Aden, and the Strait of Malacca.
  - In response to these incidences, management strategies have been put in place to combat levels of the crime such as increasing naval patrols in piracy hotspots and government schemes to deter young people from committing crime.
- **Migrant escape routes:** are another obstacle that takes place in oceans worldwide. Migrants and refugees travel from their home country often in the hope of moving to a country with better economic opportunities or safer living conditions without conflict or persecution.
  - One of the most common routes for migrants and refugees is from North Africa to Europe as people migrate from African countries like Libya, Tunisia, or the Sub-Sahara, or Middle Eastern countries like Syria or Pakistan.
  - Groups of migrants often travel on unsafe boats and risk drowning.
  - Routes are also often prone to human trafficking networks and pirates, putting many people's lives at risk.

Hazardous Earth

Global distribution of tectonic hazards
- **Crust:** the Earth has two main types of crust:
  - **Oceanic crust:** situated below the ocean and thinner than continental crust. This layer is made of **basalt** which is denser and ideal for subduction.
  - **Continental crust:** found beneath continents and thicker than oceanic crust. This type of crust is made of **granite** which is less dense than basalt.
- **Mantle:** the thickest section of all the earth's layers. (approx. 2,900 km) and made from semi-molten rock (magma).
- **Core:** broken down into two further layers (inner and outer) which are both made from **nickel** and **iron**. The inner core is a solid and the hottest part of the Earth, whereas the outer core is liquid matter.
- Tectonic plates are large rigid slabs of the Earth's upper mantle and crust. They are constantly moving and vary in size. The major plates are the Pacific, Eurasian, African, North American, South American, Indo-Australian, and Antarctic.
- Tectonic hazards such as earthquakes and volcanoes mainly occur along plate margins where the different tectonic plates meet.
- Both **destructive** (oceanic plate subducting beneath a continental plate) and **constructive** (plates moving apart) boundaries can produce earthquakes and volcanic eruptions.
- Tectonic activity is **unevenly distributed** across the globe, with some regions (e.g. parts of Asia, the Americas, and Oceania) experiencing far more hazards than others due to their position along active plate boundaries.

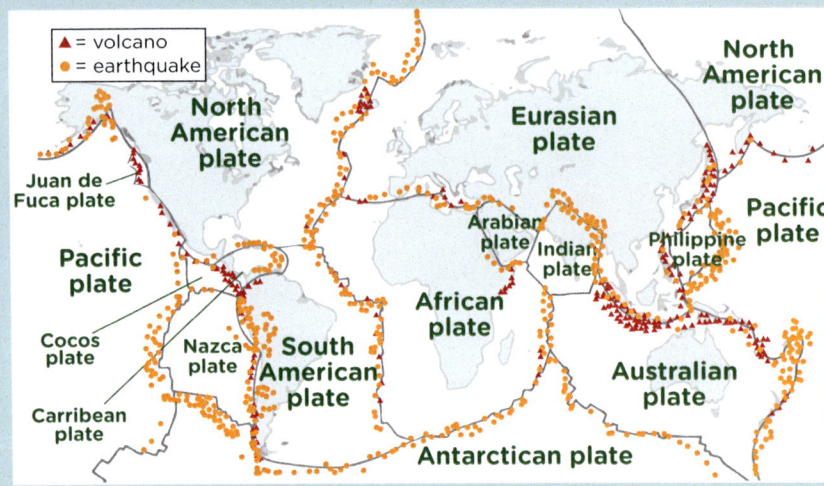

Tectonic plate boundaries
- **Convergent plate boundaries (plates move towards each other)**
  - **Oceanic-continental:** when an oceanic and continental plate converge, the denser oceanic plate subducts (sinks) under the continental plate. This forms a trench and rift valley at the point of subduction. As they converge, the rock of the continental plate crumples under pressure. As the oceanic plate subducts, it melts and rises. This is often linked to volcanoes with explosive eruptions. An example of this is the Nazca plate subducting beneath the South American plate forming the Andes mountains and Peru trench.
  - **Oceanic-oceanic:** when two oceanic plates converge, the denser one subducts. This forms an ocean trench. As the sinking plate melts, magma rises and pushes upwards forming chains of volcanoes and islands called island arcs. An example of this is the Pacific plate subducting under the Philippine plate, forming the Mariana trench.
  - **Continental-continental:** continental plates have very similar densities meaning little subduction can occur. This means they push towards each other. This is how the Alps mountains formed due to the convergence of the African and Eurasian plates.

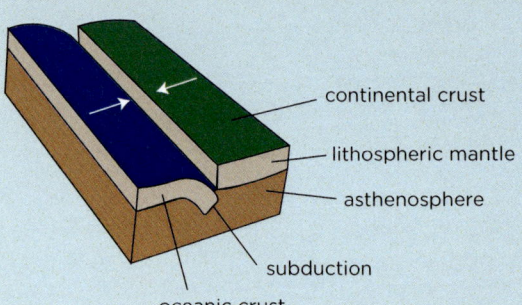

- **Divergent plate boundaries (plates move away from each other):** as plates diverge, magma can rise to the surface where it solidifies, and a mid-ocean ridge forms to create a new ocean floor (e.g. the Mid-Atlantic Ridge). Rift valleys can also form when the plates move apart and stretch, creating faults as the central block sinks downwards and creates steep-sided valleys. This stretching can cause earthquakes and volcanoes.

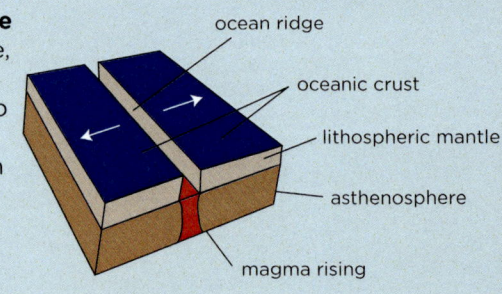

- **Conservative plate boundaries (plates slide past each other):** plates moving past each other can cause friction in certain areas. This leads to a build-up of pressure that is released through powerful earthquakes when the energy is released as seismic waves. An example of this is the San Andreas fault.

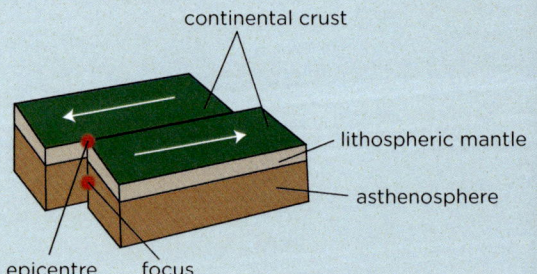

Hazardous Earth

Theories of continental drift and plate tectonics

Evidence of plate tectonics and Pangaea

Alfred Wegener claimed that continents were once joined in a supercontinent called **Pangaea**, which later drifter apart to their current positions. Initial lack of evidence caused scepticism amongst scientists, however further understanding of convection currents has led to the current theory of plate tectonics.

- **Sea floor spreading**
  - **Palaeomagnetism:** as new oceanic crust forms at mid-ocean ridges, magnetic minerals in the rock align with the Earth's magnetic field of that time. Earth's magnetic field periodically reverses its polarity, which can be seen in its alternating pattern of stripes on either side of the ridges. The symmetry of this pattern indicates that new crust is continuously forming and moving outwards: strong evidence for sea floor spreading.
  - **Age of sea floor rocks:** evidence shows that younger oceanic rock is found at mid ocean ridges, then it progressively gets older further from the ridges. This supports sea floor spreading as new crust forms and spreads outwards.
- **Geological evidence:** evidence of glaciation in Australia, India, South Africa, and Antarctica suggests that there was a time when the continents were joined (Pangaea) and have since drifted apart. The shape of continents also suggests they were once joined as they fit together.
- **Fossil evidence:** fossil species such as the Mesosaurus and Glossopteris have been found in South America, Africa, Australia, and India, now divided by vast oceans. This suggests these landmasses were once connected then developed their own evolutionary pathways after continental drift occurred.

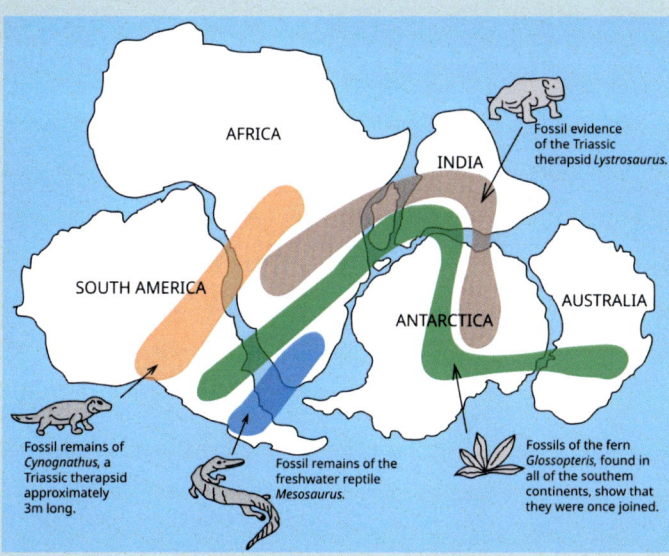

Coping with risks of tectonic hazards

- **Changes in frequency of tectonic hazards:** the frequency of tectonic activity cannot increase, decrease or be reduced. However, hazards can be mitigated and predicted. Deaths and other social impacts are more likely to occur in low-income developing countries, whereas economic loss is more likely in developed countries where land and buildings are more financially valuable.
- **Disaster risk equation:**

$$\text{Risk} = \frac{\text{magnitude of hazard} \times \text{vulnerability}}{\text{capacity to cope}}$$

  - **Hazard** refers to the probability of a disaster.
  - **Vulnerability** refers to factors such as poverty and development which may put people at risk.
  - **Capacity** to cope refers to the resources available (such as warning systems and emergency services) in the event of a disaster.
- **The relationship between disaster and response:** disasters disrupt normal conditions, causing a decline in quality of life, which prompts immediate and long-term responses. Effective, rapid response can shorten recovery time and reduce overall impact. Recovery depends on factors like preparedness, resources, governance, and hazard severity.
- **The Park model** is a graph showing how quality of life changes after a hazard event.
  - **Pre-disaster stage:** quality of life is normal; preparedness measures are in place.
  - **Disruption:** event occurs; immediate drop in quality of life.
  - **Relief phase:** emergency response (rescue, aid, shelter).
  - **Rehabilitation:** temporary infrastructure and basic services restored.
  - **Reconstruction:** long-term rebuilding; possibility of future improvement beyond pre-disaster stage with greater preparedness.

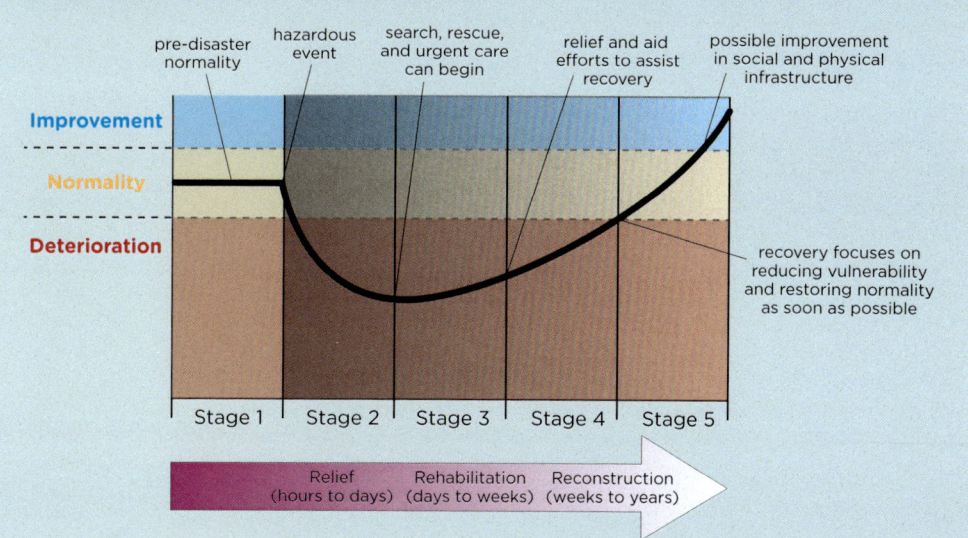

Hazardous Earth

Volcanic activity and resultant landforms

Explosive eruptions (destructive plate boundaries)	Effusive eruptions (constructive plate boundaries)	Intra plate eruptions (hotspots)
• Subduction causes gas build up in magma. When this pressure is released, eruptions are explosive. • Magma easily traps gas due to its silica and high viscosity. • Can form pyroclastic flows, steep sided stratovolcanoes, and calderas (e.g. Mt St Helens eruption, 1980).	• When low viscosity basaltic magma reaches the surface and doesn't contain gas, the lava can flow quickly over the ground in a relatively gentle, non-explosive manner. • Forms gently sloping shield volcanoes that erupt more frequently (e.g. Kilauea volcano).	• Plumes of hot magma not at plate boundaries melts/thins the lithosphere before eventually erupting. • Tectonic plates drift over the stationary plume forming a chain of extinct volcanoes (e.g. the Hawaiian Islands).

- **Volcanic Explosivity Index (VEI):** a scale used to measure the magnitude and intensity of volcanic eruptions. The scale is logarithmic and ranges from 0 (least explosive) to 8 (most explosive). A typical effusive eruption of Kilauea volcano measures 0 on the scale, whereas the Mount St Helens 1980 eruption measured 5.
- **Super-volcanoes:** volcanoes that have had an eruption that measures 8 in the VEI, meaning it erupts over 1,000 km³ of material in one eruption. For example, Yellowstone is a super-volcano that last erupted ~631,000 years ago.

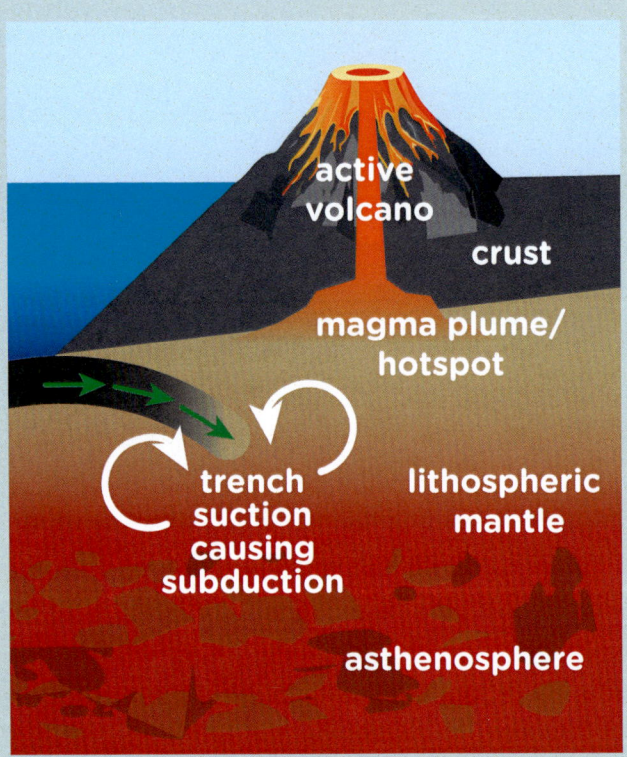

Managing volcanic hazards

Hazard	Description
Lava flows	Streams of molten rock. The speed and distance of the flow depends on the viscosity of the lava (e.g. basaltic lava flows faster and further). They destroy everything but are usually slow enough to allow for evacuation.
Pyroclastic flows	Extremely hot (500°C), rapid flow of gas, ash, and rock down the volcano's sides, incinerating everything in its path, posing an extreme risk to life.
Gas emissions	The vast volume of certain gases released in volcanic eruptions such as carbon dioxide and sulphur dioxide can cause pollution when mixed with rain (acid rain) and respiratory issues in nearby settlements.
Tephra and ash	Tephra is material blown into the air during an eruption. This may include large rocks or heavy ashfall that smothers local towns and agriculture.
Floods	Volcanic heat released during eruptions can cause rapid melting of ice or glaciers. Water can flow rapidly into towns, destroying buildings and land.
Lahars	Fast flowing, thick mudflows of ash, rock, and water, forming when material mixes with floodwater or heavy rainfall. They bury everything in their path.
Tsunamis	Volcanic activity can trigger tectonic movements of the seafloor that cause sudden displacement of water. This generates large waves that grow in height as they approach the coastline. When they reach land, they can cause many fatalities and destruction of land.

Volcanic activity occurs in multiple regions around the world. Preventative measure can be put in place to cope with the effects however these vary by country.

Strategy	Italy (AC)	Indonesia (EDC)
Attempts to mitigate the event	• Diverting lava flows help to protect buildings and settlements. • Concrete blocks can be used to redirect the flow of lava.	• Mitigating the event is limited in Indonesia due to the eruption style of volcanoes.
Attempt to mitigate vulnerability	• Advanced technology used to monitor volcanoes by the Italian National Institute of Geophysics and Volcanology. • Predictions can be made including the magnitude and exclusion zones.	• The Centre for Volcanology and Geological Hazard Mitigation in Indonesia monitor over 60 volcanoes. • Technology is not as advanced in developing countries due to limited economic funding.
Attempts to mitigate loss	• Rapid response plans in place involving emergency services to reduce deaths and injuries. • Evacuation plans in place.	• Emergency shelters are prepared in case of eruption. • Emergency services are equipped. • Aid is supplied to those affected however rural communities can be much harder to access.

Hazardous Earth

Earthquake activity and resultant landforms

Earthquakes are caused by the release of built-up tension at plate margins, mid ocean ridges, collision zones or ocean trenches, causing waves of vibrations and rapid shaking of the Earth's crust.

- **Shallow focus earthquakes:** occur at depths of 0-70 km, are commonly low energy but is they are high energy the impacts can be very severe as the energy released is closer to the surface.
- **Deep focus earthquakes:** occur at depths of 70 km+ and are rarely destructive. High temperatures at greater depth means rock is melted and more unlikely to cause faults.
- **Seismic waves:**
  - **P-waves (primary):** fast travelling, low frequency waves that vibrate in the direction of travel.
  - **S-waves (secondary):** slower, more high frequency waves that vibrate perpendicular to the direction of travel.
  - **Surface waves:** slowest type of wave, travel through the Earth's surface and are cause the most damage.

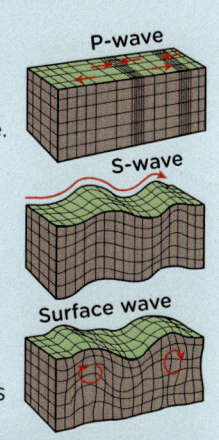

Methods of measuring earthquake magnitude and intensity

Richter scale	Moment magnitude scale	Modified Mercalli scale
• Measures magnitude using the height of waves on a seismograph. • Logarithmic scale (each number on the scale is a x10 increase in amplitude). • Does not account for damage and can inaccurately represent magnitude of very large earthquakes.	• Measures magnitude of earthquakes more accurately than the Richter scale, especially for larger earthquakes. • Most widely used by scientists today. • Largest recorded was the Japan earthquake in 2011, at 9.0.	• Measures intensity as well as impact on the population, environment and buildings. • Scale from I – X (Roman numerals) ranking from not felt to extreme. • More subjective than other scales.

- **Effects of earthquakes on landforms and landscapes:**
  - **Escarpments:** sudden vertical displacement along a fault during an earthquake can create or heighten fault scarps (steep slopes or cliffs). These are common at transform and normal faults, where differential uplift or subsidence occurs. For example, the 1959 Hebgen Lake earthquake (Montana, USA) created a scarp up to 6.7 m high.
  - **Rift valleys:** form when crust is stretched and pulled apart by extensional tectonics, with earthquakes accompanying fault movement. Faulting produces parallel cracks (fault lines) and subsidence of central blocks, creating elongated depressions. For example, the East African Rift Valley is shaped by ongoing seismic and tectonic activity.

Managing earthquake hazards

Hazards	Description
Ground shaking	The seismic waves during an earthquake cause vibration that make the ground shake. Earthquakes of higher magnitude generate stronger shaking. Weaker geology can also cause more ground movement and displacement. During horizontal shaking, buildings and infrastructure are most at risk and can be subject to collapse. This can cause fatalities and injuries as well as damage to services such as water and electricity.
Liquefaction	Occurs when earthquakes cause loose, saturated material to lose integral strength and behave like liquids. This leads structures above it to collapse and can cause widespread damage.
Landslides and avalanches	Intense ground shaking can cause the mass movement of soil or snow down sloping land which can lead to mudslides, rockfalls and avalanches in cold regions. These hazards are dangerous as they happen quickly and can bury settlements and people in debris. They also block roads, railways, and other important infrastructure (e.g. the 2015 Nepal earthquake caused 21,000+ landslides).
Tsunamis	Displacement of a large volume of water causing tall, powerful waves that grow in height as they approach shore, caused by rapid uplifting of the seabed when a tectonic plate is jolted out of position during earthquakes. This can also cause underwater/submarine landslides when earthquakes displace sediment, generating large waves.

Strategy	Japan	Nepal
Attempt to mitigate vulnerability	• Japan Meteorological Agency provides information to people prior to and in the event of earthquakes. • Building infrastructure that is resistant to earthquake tremors, including counterweights and flexible steel frames. • Warning systems for tsunamis and earthquakes to warn people and evacuate them accordingly.	• National Society for Earthquake Technology helps to identify most at-risk zones, improve building standards and spread awareness through education programmes.
Attempts to mitigate loss	• Japan has extensive resources and plans in place to limit the losses caused in the event of earthquakes. • Funding for reconstruction is available for rapid recovery.	• International aid supplied by organisations/charities to support emergency services that are often under strain in disasters.

Hazardous Earth

Responses to volcanic activity

Populations exist in areas of volcanic activity despite the risks of living there. The reasons for why vary between levels of development.

	Mt Ontake, Japan	Mt Merapi, Indonesia
Background	• Japan is an extremely tectonically active region. • Mt Ontake is a stratovolcano that last erupted in October 2014 killing 63 people.	• Indonesia is an extremely tectonically active region. • Mt Merapi is a stratovolcano that last erupted in January 2024, however one of its most sever eruptions occurred in November 2010 killing 341 people.
Why do people live there?	• Populations have existed near Mt Ontake for centuries meaning people have long-term cultural and familial connections. • The high fertility soils surrounding volcanoes supports local communities and agriculture. • Tradition and spirituality has developed, with the volcano being a core part of people's beliefs. • Local economy is supported by the tourism of people attracted to the scenic landscape.	• Many Indonesian people live near Mt Merapi because of limited economic resources to move elsewhere. • Fertile soils support agriculture and subsistence farming that form the basis of many local communities. • The area also has traditional and spiritual significance for many people.
Economic impact of eruption	• Loss of tourism revenue as the area was deemed unsafe and many of the people killed were tourist hikers.	• Crop failure and death of livestock caused many communities fall into economic struggle. • Support from aid was sent to support affected individuals.
Environmental impact	• Large areas of land were covered in ash and affected by pyroclastic flows. This has damaging impacts on vegetation and wildlife whilst also impacting agriculture.	• Ash fall buried villages and polluted rivers. • Pyroclastic flows, lahars, and acid rain destroyed nearby settlements and forests.

Responses to earthquake activity

As with volcanoes, populations exist in areas of earthquake activity despite the risks of living there, in both developed and less developed regions.

	Tohoku, Japan	Ghorka, Nepal
Background	• In 2011, an earthquake of 9.0 Mw affected Japan with its epicentre 130 km east of Sendai. • The earthquake and subsequent tsunami caused the death of an estimated 18,500 people.	• In 2015, an earthquake of 7.3 Mw occurred in Nepal 76 km from Kathmandu. • The death toll was over 8,500 and nearly 16,800 injured people.
Why do people live there?	• Japan experiences frequent tectonic activity meaning people have adapted and most are low magnitude. • Japan is an economic hub that provides employment opportunities and prosperity. • Lots of Japan has earthquake resistant infrastructure that makes people feel safer.	• Many people have strong ancestral ties to Nepal and earthquakes. • Earthquakes are often not severe. • Some residents do not understand the risk of living in tectonically active regions.
Economic impact of earthquake	• Estimated $360 billion in property damage. • 45,700 properties damaged. • Fukushima Daiichi nuclear incident caused the meltdown of three reactors.	• $10 billion worth of damage. • Many areas had to rely on foreign aid in the aftermath of the earthquake. • Tourism industry was affected.
Environmental impact	• Tsunami caused widespread damage to buildings and the landscape. • Radiation leaks from the nuclear powerplant damaged wildlife and contaminated the environment, requiring an exclusion zone.	• Landslides and avalanches caused because of tremors.

Climate change

Historic changes in Earth's climate

The historic changes of Earth's climate can be analysed using methods like:
- **Marine and lake sediments:** Sediment layers at the bottom of oceans hold small fossils that contain chemical isotopes that reveal the temperature of the climate when they formed. In lake sediments, different pollen and spores suggest what vegetation existed at that time which in turn indicates what the climate was like.
- **Ice cores:** ice cores contain isotopes of hydrogen and oxygen in small air bubbles which can also be analysed. The frequency of certain isotopes indicates the temperature when the ice formed.
- **Tree rings:** the width of tree rings that grow each year varies with climate. Wide rings suggest there was a warmer, wetter climate when it formed, thin rings suggest colder and/or drier conditions.
- **Fossils:** the fossil remains of plants and animals indicate the climate in which they were able to survive. Some species would only have been able to withstand specific conditions which allows scientists to identify the exact details of climate at the time.

The past climate of Earth:
- **100 million years ago:** Earth began its transition from a greenhouse to an icehouse. Before this, global temperatures were 6-8 degrees warmer than today, meaning no polar ice caps existed and sea levels were much higher.
- **35 million years ago:** temperatures dropped and ice sheets formed in Antarctica. This process was encouraged by the rapid fall in carbon in the atmosphere, as well as the geographic isolation of Antarctica from South America and Australia during continental drift.
- **2 million years ago:** the Quaternary period began, characterised by alternating periods of cold glacial periods (typically lasting 100,000 years) and warmer interglacial periods (typically lasting 10,000-15,000 years). During glacial periods, temperatures fell and much of Earth was covered in continental ice sheets.
- **11,700 years ago:** the current Holocene period began. This is an interglacial period with warmer temperatures and occasional periods of cooler or warmer climates.

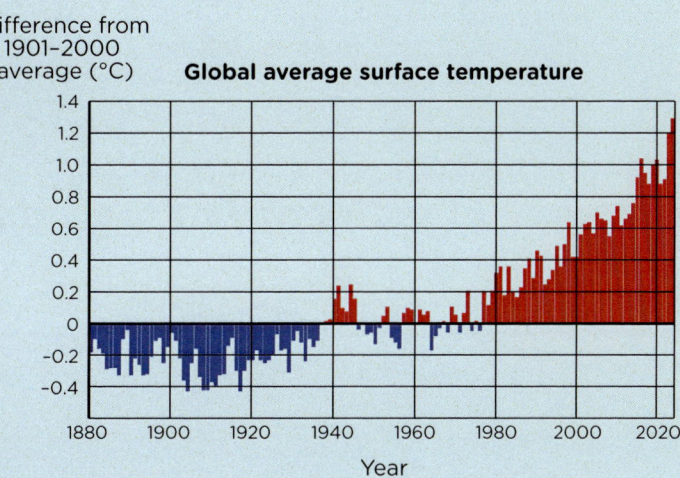

Natural forces that have influenced climate change
- **Plate tectonics:**
  - Continental drift can cause changes in climate. When landmasses are focused at polar regions, ice sheets form which lead to the cooling of Earth's climate. On the other hand, when land is clustered around the equator, climate warms.
  - Volcanic eruptions can also change the climate. The large clouds of ash cause temporary cooling of the climate due to blocking solar radiation. In the long term, the release of carbon dioxide and methane enhances the greenhouse effect which causes global warming.
- **Milankovitch cycles:**
  - Scientist Milutin Milankovitch suggested that cycles of Earth's eccentricity, obliquity and precession may explain changes in solar energy received by Earth and therefore explain patterns of climate change.
  - Eccentricity refers to the shape of Earth's orbit. Over the span of around 100,000 years, the orbit shifts from circular to more elliptical (oval).
  - Obliquity refers to the tilt of Earth on its axis. Around every 41,000 years, the angle of tilt changes. Larger tilting means seasons are more extreme.
  - Precession refers to the wobble of Earth on its axis. This cycle lasts around 26,000 years and impacts the timings of seasons because of gravitational pull and tides.

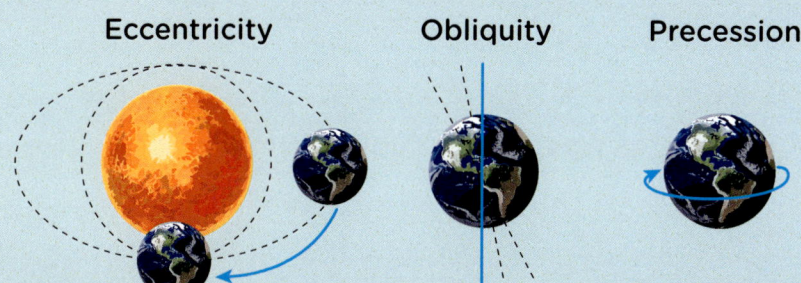

- **Solar output:**
  - The amount of energy the sun emits is not constant, yet it varies over time. Changes in sunspot activity is linked to climate change.
  - More sunspots correlate to greater solar output and warmer climate compared to fewer sunspots, less solar output and cooler climates on Earth.
- **Natural atmospheric greenhouse gases:**
  - Greenhouse gases such as methane, carbon dioxide and water vapour absorb the Sun's radiation and re-radiate it, causing warmer climates.
  - Positive feedback loops such as melting permafrost and warmer oceans releasing more carbon into the atmosphere means warming continues.

Climate change

The Anthropocene

The Anthropocene is a term for the current geological epoch where human activity has become the presiding force that influences Earth's climate.

Evidence of global warming since the 19th century	
Increases in surface, atmospheric, and ocean temperatures	Global average surface temperatures have increased since the late 1800s. Since 1900, average surface temperature has increased by 1°C. Ocean temperatures have also increased, leading to more ice melting and less carbon stored in oceans.
Shrinking valley glaciers and ice cover	From 1979 to 2024, the extent of ice coverage decreased by 12.1% each decade on average. Ice is retreating earlier in summer and reforming later into winter months.
Rising sea level	Sea levels have risen since the late nineteenth century. As the climate becomes warmer, ice sheets and other stores in the cryosphere begin to melt. This rises relative sea level. Warmer oceans cause thermal expansion, where water expands as it gets warmer.
Increasing atmospheric water vapour	Increasing temperatures means more water vapour forms due to the increasing rate of evaporation. This exacerbates the issue of rising temperatures further by enhancing the greenhouse effect.

Why have greenhouse gas emissions increased since the pre-industrial era?
- The process of industrialisation required enormous amounts of energy. The introduction of large power stations, forms of transport, and other industries involved the burning of damaging amounts of fossil fuels.
- Population began to increase rapidly meaning consumption and demand for resources rose.
- Continued reliance on non-renewable resources like gas, oil and coal despite the introduction of renewable energy sources.
- Deforestation due to clearing land for agriculture or industry for example meant that the number of trees that could undertake photosynthesis decreased rapidly and released carbon stored in its biomass.
- In the beginning of the industrial revolution in the 1900s, greenhouse gases were mainly emitted by the USA or countries in Europe. More recently, this trend has declined however countries in Asia, especially India and China, have taken over as emitting the most GHGs in line with their growth in industry and need for energy.
- **Enhanced greenhouse effect:** human activity has added large volumes of greenhouse gases to the atmosphere, far beyond the natural greenhouse effect. As a result, more solar radiation is trapped and re-radiated, causing the atmosphere to warm.

Responses to climate change

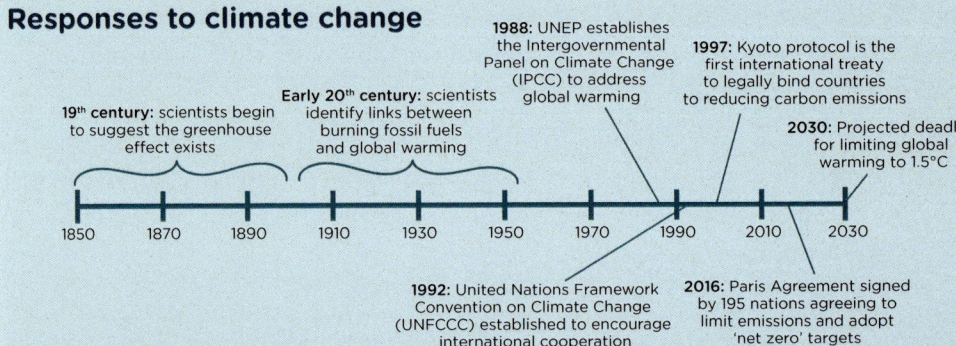

- **The role of governments and international organisations:**
  - **The EU:** has several policies such as the EU Emissions Trading System aimed at reducing carbon emissions, with a 2040 target of reducing emissions by 90% from 1990 levels.
  - **The UN:** the UNFCCC initiated the Kyoto Protocol, involving countries in reducing their emissions by a 5% reduction below levels in 1990 by 2012. Despite this, major emitters like China and the USA did not join the agreement.
  - **The UK:** the 2008 Climate Change Act is a legally binding target of net zero emissions by 2050 through investments in renewable energy and carbon budgets.
- **The role of the media and possible bias in shaping public opinion:**
  - Bias exists within all forms of media. Left wing outlets tend to address the urgency of climate change, whereas right wing outlets are often sceptical and downplay severity.
  - Headlines often portray exaggerated information that focus on certain negative points, misinterpreted science, or falsely balance the reality of climate change.
  - Different interest groups also have contrasting aims. Industries that rely on fossil fuels often want to protect profits and downplay the severity of climate change.
- **Future emission scenarios:**
  - There are four main **representative concentration pathways** (RCPs) which suggest different scenarios for climate change, ranging from the least (RCP 2.6) to most damaging (RCP 2.8) depending on whether greenhouse gas emissions continue to increase.

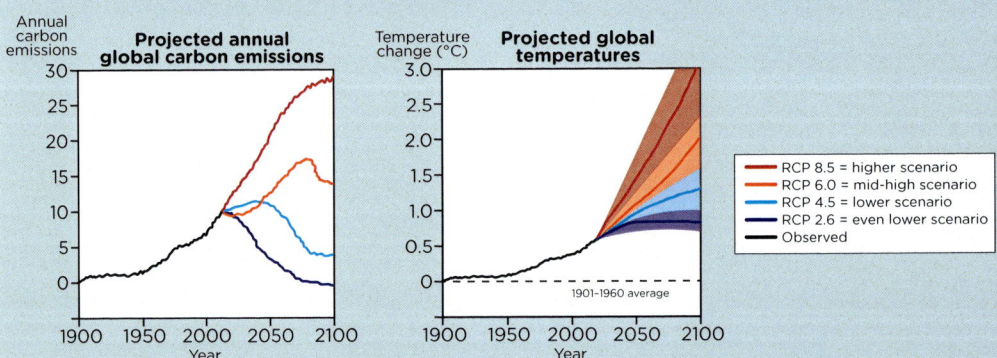

Climate change

Impacts of climate change

- **Impacts on health:**
  - As heatwaves become more severe, heat related deaths and illnesses increase.
  - Diseases such as malaria survive in warmer conditions. As previously unaffected regions' temperature increases, these diseases can spread.
  - Extreme weather conditions have a major impact on food security. Flooding and droughts can destroy crops, leading to more famine and undernutrition if sufficient food can no longer be supplied.
- **Impacts on ecosystems:**
  - Increasing frequency of droughts can cause wildfires which destroy habitats and reduce the carbon stored in vegetation.
  - In Arctic regions, reduction in sea ice damages habitats for polar animals.
  - Migration patterns of birds is also changing in response to climate change. As weather conditions become more extreme and unpredictable, migratory birds are forced to adapt their journeys to suit their survival needs.
  - Global warming leads to increasing ocean temperatures. This disrupts marine life as they may have to migrate to areas that better suit their survival needs. This has a knock-on effect on food chains, causing damage to many other species.
  - Ocean acidification causes coral bleaching which can damage and kill reef structures, harming other marine organisms in the ecosystem.
- **Impacts on extreme weather:**
  - Heatwaves become more frequent with climate change, exacerbating the risk of wildfires. Areas of Europe and North America are most affected.
  - Flash flooding is also a risk associated with sudden, intense rainfall. Parts of Europe are seeing more flash floods, and many coastal countries and cities may suffer from flooding due to storm surges and rising sea levels.
  - As some regions become much drier, droughts occur more often and intensely. This is mainly in dryland regions such as the Sahel or California.
  - Tropical storms (hurricanes, cyclones and typhoons) become more intense as warmer oceans and higher rainfall.
- **Impacts on vulnerable groups of people:**
  - Elderly people and young children are more vulnerable to health conditions related to heat such as heat stroke.
  - Rural communities: are often self-sufficient and rely on agriculture and traditional practices to provide food and water. This is very vulnerable to droughts, flooding and unpredictable weather patterns.
  - Indigenous groups that live in vulnerable environments such as Arctic tundra or rainforests are impacted by the effect of climate change on these areas and often lack the resources to adapt.
  - Populations in coastal regions are likely to be more vulnerable to sea level rise and extreme tropical storms, erosion and storm surges.
- **Impacts on vulnerable environments:**
  - Semi-arid regions: rainfall is likely to become less frequent meaning droughts are more severe and desertification occurs.
  - Arctic tundra: global warming leads to the melting of permafrost, releasing stored carbon and encouraging the growth of more vegetation and forests.
  - Rainforests: temperatures may increase and a fall in precipitation means rainforests could become much drier.

Mitigation and adaptation in response to climate change

Mitigation strategies are those that try to reduce the impacts of climate change

Strategy	Description
Energy efficiency and conservation	Reducing the amount of energy consumed and wasted such as by improving efficiency of buildings through insulation, windows, and renewable sources of energy. The UK government offers financial support and incentives for implementing these in homes.
Low carbon energy sources	Transitioning from non-renewable energy (coil, oil and gas) to nuclear power or renewable sources like solar, geothermal, and wind.
Carbon capture and storage	Capturing CO_2 at the source and transporting it deep underground so it doesn't enter the atmosphere. May be successful but requires high costs and requires lots of energy.
Forestry	Reducing deforestation and increasing afforestation/reforestation programmes means more carbon can be removed from the atmosphere by photosynthesis and stored in the biosphere.
Geoengineering	Engineering solutions have been proposed which utilise technology to reduce climate change. For example, reducing the amount of solar radiation using large reflective surfaces on the ground or in obit.

Adaptation strategies are responses that involve adjusting to impacts of climate change that are already taking place.

- **The framework of adaptation:**
  - **Retreat:** relocate vulnerable communities away from areas at risk. For example, this could involve moving people living along coastlines vulnerable to flooding and sea level rise to safer, inland areas.
  - **Accommodate:** adjust and change current processes to better deal with the effects of climate change. This may be through developing new methods of agriculture to ensure better preparedness for famine and drought.
  - **Protect:** can be in the form of physical barriers that defend against threats of climate change (e.g. flood levees, fire breaks) or socio-economic safety nets to ensure people affected by climate change are supported.
- **What adaptation looks like:**
  - In flood prone areas, many buildings are built on stilts to prevent damage. More green areas in cities and on rooftops to increase interception and slow down surface run off.
  - Improved insulation to reduce reliance on energy usage and heating in colder months.
  - Installing shading and ventilation to limit the need for air conditioning.
- **The role of geopolitics in the human response to climate change:**
  - IPCC releases scientific reports outlining predictions for future climate changes, impacts and possible responses.
  - International directives such as the Kyoto Protocol have had ranging levels of success. The Kyoto Protocol was achieved by many countries, reducing their carbon emissions by over 5% below 1990 levels, however the biggest emitters were not involved meaning overall success was limited.
  - Policies also exist at national and sub-national levels (e.g. the UK's Climate Change Act and emission targets).

Changing spaces and places

Place identity and perception
- **Space:** locations that have no meaning attached to them.
- **Place:** a space with an attached meaning, this can be shaped by experiences, memories, or perceptions of place. The concept of place is subjective and varies between people. Place identity involves a wide range of physical, demographic, built, cultural, political and socioeconomic factors.
  - Formal representations of place: data-based, objective measures (e.g. census data, crime statistics, geospatial data).
  - Informal representations of place: subjective or creative interpretations of place (e.g. TV shows, art, film, music, literature, photography, graffiti).

Comparing two place profiles:

	Camden Town, London (urban, global city)	Totnes, Devon (rural, small market town)
Demographics	Diverse, young population with high migrant presence	Older, stable population with recent influx of eco-conscious migrants
Culture	Vibrant arts and music scene; historic markets	Strong local heritage, eco-friendly initiatives
Politics	Local governance focused on urban regeneration and housing	Active community groups influence local planning
Socio-economic	Mixed wealth; pockets of deprivation alongside affluent areas	Mixed economy; tourism, agriculture, small businesses dominate
Natural characteristics	Regent's Canal, small parks	Surrounded by countryside, rivers, and woodland
Built characteristics	Victorian terraces, modern apartments, cultural venues	Historic buildings, conservation areas
Past and present connections	• Historically industrial, now a cultural hub attracting tourists and creatives • Connected via London's transport network regionally and internationally • Global influence from migration and cultural exchanges	• Historically a market town with agricultural ties • Connected regionally by road and rail; international links via tourism • Embedded in global sustainability networks (transition town movement)

Factors influencing perceptions of place
- **Age:**
  - People of different ages experience places differently because changing different needs and interpretations.
  - Even as people age, the requirements of place are often similar between people. For example, a park may be a fun place for a child to play, as well as a pleasant place for athletic adults to exercise or elderly people to go on walks, so many people prioritise living near parks for their families and wellbeing.
- **Gender:**
  - Places are perceived differently by each gender. Safety, accessibility, or societal factors impact how men and women interact with space. For example, women may feel less safe in cities at night because of fear of crime.
- **Sexuality:**
  - Members of the LGBTQ+ community may also perceive certain spaces differently.
  - Some places may be perceived as more threatening to people's identity, whereas others may feel safer where people can be themselves.
  - Lots of urban centres have areas where members of LGBTQ+ cluster and feel accepted (e.g. bars and clubs in Soho, London).
- **Religion:**
  - For some, places of worship hold no personal meaning whereas for others they may be a crucial part of their lives and spirituality.
  - For example, churches, mosques, temples, synagogues, and cathedrals are all buildings that mark religious significance for large groups of people and can be found across the world.
- **Role:**
  - People's role in different settings influences their use and perception of a place.
  - For example, a waiter or waitress may perceive a restaurant very differently whilst working than they would whilst having a celebratory meal with friends or family.
  - Emotional attachments to places can develop because of memories, experiences, family, religion, culture and more. These factors often cause people to develop strong connections to places, such as those attached to childhood memories or significant life events.
- **Globalisation:**
  - Globalisation is the increasing interconnectedness of people, commerce, and cultures across the world because of advancing technology, transport, and communication making flows of ideas and people much faster.
  - Because of globalisation, the concept of **'time-space compression'** arose, where the perceived distance between places feels smaller. People can interact and travel between places very quickly because factors such as the internet, media and travel. This can bring diversity to urban areas, introducing new cultures, food, languages, and religions which enrich perceptions of place.
  - However, globalisation can also result in a loss of place identity as TNCs and brands are ubiquitous and homogenous, making many places seem familiar regardless of location.

Changing spaces and places

Distribution of resources, wealth, and opportunities across places

Housing	Healthcare	Education	Employment	Income
• Includes the quality, affordability, and ownership of where people live. • The disparity of some people living in safe, secure homes whilst others face homelessness and overcrowding are indicators of inequality. • Tenure refers to whether housing is owner, rented or owned with a mortgage. Ownership is an indicator of wealth as it is linked to greater financial security.	• Access to healthcare can be influenced by location, income or services. • Deprived areas often have limited access to healthcare services or fewer medical centres available to them. • Unsafe living environments, poverty, poor sanitation, and insufficient access to water and food can also impact health. • This can be measured by the ratio of doctors per 1000 people or life expectancy for example.	• The ability of everyone to access learning and educational opportunities. Education and literacy is key to ending poverty and improving employment. • Can be measured through literacy level or qualifications. Despite this, formal qualifications are not always indicative of education as traditional knowledge or informal education are more common.	• Regular and secure employment is linked to income and stability. • Unemployment or insufficient income can cause social inequalities as it means people may have to live in poor quality housing or are unable to afford sufficient, healthy food.	• Inequality in income can be measured using the Gini coefficient on a decimal scale from 0-1 where lower scores indicate low levels of income inequality. • Rising costs of living can have a damaging impact on households and their ability to afford essentials like food and shelter.

Placemaking process of rebranding

Places may rebrand in order to regenerate 'run down' areas and give them a new sense of place and identity, to attract tourism, to attract investment, to redevelop an area that suffers from the effects of deindustrialisation, or to improve quality of life.

Strategies for rebranding places:
- **Sport:** hosting sporting events and tournaments can attract large amounts of media attention, tourism, and investment which greatly support the rebranding of an area.
- **Art:** art installations, exhibitions, galleries, and street art (e.g. Banksy in Bristol).
- **Heritage:** restoring historical landmarks and buildings can rebrand places by attracting tourism and enhancing their cultural value.
- **Retail:** shopping centres, flagship stores, and improving customer experience.
- **Architecture:** new buildings or restoring historical buildings.
- **Food:** markets, restaurants, cafes, especially with new food options (e.g. Camden Market in London is known for its plethora of international foods).

Stakeholders involved in the process of rebranding
- **Government:** help to plan and provide funding for rebranding projects.
- **EU:** identify areas that are most deprived and in need of regeneration and provide financial support through the European Regional Development Fund (ERDF).
- **NGOs:** charities and non-profit organisations help to support local regeneration of buildings, infrastructure and communities.
- **Corporate bodies:** provide investment for regeneration projects and develop business through opening new stores, offices and commercial spaces.

One issue of rebranding is that it is not always supported by everyone. Rebranding can often diminish the original identity, tradition or culture of a place leaving communities alienated. Gentrification can also occur where local residents are forced to move away as regeneration caused the cost of living in that area increases.

Social inequality and structural economic change

- **Social inequality:** the uneven distribution of opportunities, wealth and resources within and between places and societies.
- During the first wave of industrialisation, factories and manufacturing processes were centred in advanced countries. Over time and as de-industrialisation occurred, large TNCs began to outsource these processes to countries where labour and costs were cheaper. This caused large-scale unemployment for the primary and secondary sector workers in ACs and there was a shift towards tertiary and quaternary service jobs such as finance and IT. This can be illustrated using the **Clark Fisher model**, shown on the right.

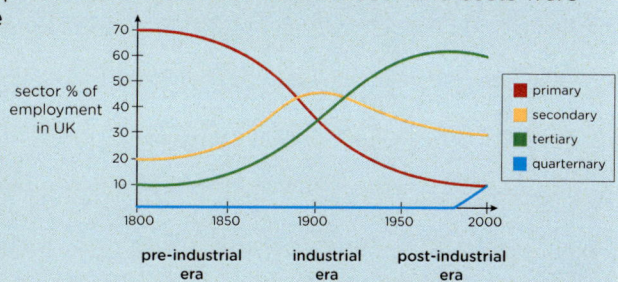

- **Positive impacts of structural economic change:**
  ◦ Tertiary and quaternary sectors create high-value industries and job opportunities.
  ◦ Provided employment opportunities for LIDCs, supporting their development.
  ◦ Increased skilled workers and encourages entrepreneurship and innovation.
  ◦ Both de-industrialisation and industrialisation sectors can attract inward investment.
- **Negative impacts of structural economic change:**
  ◦ Thousands of unskilled workers in ACs became unemployed when factories closed, and manufacturing was outsourced towards LIDCs and EDCs.
  ◦ De-industrialisation left areas that relied on primary and secondary sectors (such as mining towns) deprived and with a declining economy.
  ◦ Workers may be subject to exploitation and unsafe working conditions.
  ◦ Distribution of wealth is often centred in urban areas, so inequalities still exist.

Changing spaces and places

The effect of cyclic economic change on social inequality
- **Recessions** (phases of economic decline): unemployment spikes, particularly affecting low-income workers. This increases poverty as job losses and fall in wages means people are less able to afford necessities. For those who stay in employment, disposable income decreases which has negative impacts on leisure industries and businesses that provide non-essential goods/services.
- **Booms** (phases of economic growth): increased levels of employment which helps in reducing poverty and improving standard of living. Higher wages mean people have more disposable income which supports the local economy and business owners. Wealth created during economic booms can often only be felt by high-earners or business owners for example, so wealth is not evenly distributed.

Role of the government in reducing or reinforcing social inequality:
- **Education:** by funding education, young people are provided with opportunities and skills to develop their economic stability and career.
- **Taxation:** progressive taxing (based on income) aims to redistribute wealth throughout the country. The money provided to the government from taxes is put back into the community by funding public services.
- **Subsidies:** provide financial support through housing and other means to low-income people (e.g. bursaries, free school meals, or the UK benefits system).

	New York City, USA	Dharavi, Mumbai, India
Evidence of social inequality	• Stark contrast between affluent areas (Manhattan's Upper East Side) and deprived areas (Bronx, parts of Brooklyn) • Differences in housing quality, environmental quality (air pollution higher near industrial zones), and crime rates • Digital divide: lower-income households have reduced internet access and digital literacy	• Informal settlements with overcrowded housing and poor sanitation vs. affluent business districts nearby • Low environmental quality (pollution, waste accumulation) • High crime rates linked to unemployment and lack of infrastructure
Factors influencing inequality	• Income disparity (Wall Street vs. low-wage service workers) • Ethnicity and historical segregation. • Education access varies sharply by district funding	• Low income from informal economy jobs • Limited access to healthcare, education, and clean water • Gender inequalities in employment opportunities
Impact on daily life	• Health inequalities (life expectancy can vary by 10+ years between boroughs) • Reduced mobility due to transport affordability	• Long commutes for work • Poor health outcomes from contaminated water and air • Limited digital access reduces opportunities for education and business

People influencing places
In order for placemaking to occur, a combination of different groups and players come together to shape and develop a space.

Player	Role
Architects and planners	• Designing and developing places that support a multitude of needs can help to transform places (e.g. the regeneration of Battersea power station transformed the area into a centre for business, residence, and leisure whilst maintaining iconic historical features) • Making areas accessible and safe, places can be attractive for a much wider range of communities and people • Adapting cities to provide activities and services 24 hours a day has been increasingly prioritised (e.g. introducing extended public transport services, late night retail, and reducing laws around 24-hour licensing can contribute to economic growth)
Local community groups	• Operate on a local scale through improving spaces in towns such as parks, high streets, and residential areas • Residents' associations work to address local issues (e.g. traffic, noise complaints, preserving green areas) • Increasingly prevalent on online platforms where campaigns are organised, and people can discuss issues and ideas for their areas
Local government	• Approving, supporting, and funding regeneration projects locally • Supporting local businesses and providing training • Improving infrastructure such as public transport • Developing economic hubs that attract investment and tourism (e.g. the Mayor's "Let's Do London" campaign helped to bring an extra £162 million in tourist spending in 2023)
MNCs	• Attract foreign direct investment • Stimulate economic growth through business and job opportunities
National government	• Provide budgets and funding for economic change nationally • Adapting taxation policies to better suit economic development • Implementing national scale development projects such as HS2 • Hosting global events such as the Olympics or international conferences that attract the attention of worldwide media and increase the status of countries. • Foreign Direct Investment is attracted by governments by investing in infrastructure and offering tax incentives that encourage entrepreneurship and flow of capital
International institutions	• Provide funding for regeneration projects • Support trade relationships

International trade and globalisation

International trade flows and patterns
- **International trade** is the exchange of capital, services and goods globally. Patterns of trade vary spatially and temporally whilst being subject to a range of political, social and economic factors.
- **World Trade Organization:** an organisation with 166 members that governs global trade by implementing regulations and ensuring trade is fair.
- The three main concepts of international trade:
  - **Merchandise:** involves the importing and exporting of goods (such as grains, oil or cars) between countries.
  - **Services:** intangible products that provides exchange of knowledge, labour skills and expertise. These may include financial services, education or healthcare.
  - **Capital:** relates to the movement of wealth around the world, such as land and equipment; or money, stocks and shares.

Most flows of trade occur intra-regionally:
- Within Europe, the EU facilitates the flow of goods and services by eliminating many barriers such as tariffs between members. In 2024, trade within the EU was worth €4,025 billion.
- Within Asia, similarly the ASEAN also facilitates trade between members, allowing more efficient trading of goods.

Inter-regional trading is also important:
- Trade between Asia and Europe is an inter-regional major flow. China is one of the world's largest exporters of electronic goods to the UK and other European countries.
- Trade between the USA and EU is also a prominent flow of goods, with €851 billion worth in 2023.

Human Development Index
Patterns and correlations can be identified between a country's socio-economic development and trade. The Human Development Index (HDI) can be used to measure development and Value of Exports can measure the economic worth of trade. There is a **positive correlation** between HDI and value of exports:
- USA has a HDI of 0.938 with a total value of exports of $3.05 trillion (10.22% of all global exports)
- UK has a HDI of 0.946 with a total value of exports of $1.07 trillion (3.58% of global exports)
- China has a HDI of 0.797 with a total value of exports of $3.51 trillion. China holds the highest percentage of global exports at 11.76%
- Somalia has the second lowest HDI of 0.404 with a total value of exports of $2.16 billion (0.01% of global exports)
- Although there is not a perfect positive correlation, the general pattern shows that higher HDI = higher value of exports.

Effects of international trade

	Positive effects (promoting stability, growth, and development)	**Negative effects** (inequalities, conflicts, and injustices)
Flows of people and ideas	• Migration of people helps to fill shortages in the labour market which helps to boost productivity and growth of industries. • Skilled workers also bring knowledge and expertise to destination countries which helps develop and support new businesses. However, this can lead to brain drain in the countries of origin if migrants don't return.	• Workers are often exploited for labour (including child and slave labour) meaning they are underpaid and suffer working in poor, unsafe conditions. • Work opportunities are often unequal, meaning women and unskilled workers struggle to access the same opportunities.
Money	• Revenue made from international trade increases a country's GDP, allowing the improvement of public services and gives governments funding to support a better quality of life and reduce poverty. • Foreign Direct Investment (FDI) because of international trade also supports countries in improving infrastructure and creating employment opportunities.	• Tariffs and trade policies can cause conflict between countries. • Trade is dominated by powerful countries which can lead to exploitation of labour in less powerful countries. • The benefits of trade may only reach certain regions of a country, leaving others less developed and creating more inequality.
Technology	• The improving global availability of advancing technology means that production, manufacturing and trading processes are much more efficient. • Technology has helped to increase communication between countries and businesses, meaning pinch points and weaknesses in supply chains can be identified and solved much faster. • The use of e-commerce has added convenience and increased accessibility of many markets, allowing an increase in revenue from international trade.	• Less developed countries often lack the infrastructure needed to keep up and benefit from advancing technology in trade. This means they continue to be unable to effectively compete in high value global markets. • Large businesses often locate in developed urban areas, leaving other regions at a disadvantage.

International trade and globalisation

Factors influencing access to markets

Technology, transport and communications	• Global supply chains refer to the movement of goods and services between the network of consumers, distributors, suppliers or manufacturers. • LIDCs are increasingly becoming more involved in global supply chains, aiding further development and investment. • Technology within trade markets has helped to improve the efficiency of supply chains through providing better communication and infrastructure.
Increasing influence of MNCs in EDCs	• MNCs play a large role in the international trade system. Many of these companies have factories and offices in EDCs like India. • Many MNCs outsource to cut costs or to increase their work force. Some EDCs also offer incentives to companies to invest their businesses in their countries. • This has benefits such as bringing investment and employment opportunities to the host country, allowing development and raising of living standards. • There also negative aspects: workers in less developed countries may be forced to work for low wages in unsafe conditions because sufficient safeguarding regulations aren't in place, pollution from factories have harmful impacts on their environment and governments often have little control over how the businesses operate.
Regional trading blocs	• Aim to facilitate easier access to trade markets by reducing tariffs and other trade barriers. Membership to these trade blocs encourages investment and intra-regional trading (e.g. EU, ASEAN, NAFTA). • The EU is a single market trading bloc which allows the free movement of trade between its member states. The EU also develops trading relationships with external countries to increase investment, economic growth, and market expansion.
Growth of 'south-south' trade	• This refers to the rise in trade between EDCs and LIDCs, mainly due to the rising economic power of EDCs such as China and Brazil. • This has allowed more countries to access international trading markets.
Growth of services in the global economy	• There is a global trend in the growth in trade of services like finance and IT. • ACs have been the top exporters of services, however, recently there has been a rapid rise in LIDCs exporting services. This helps to attract investment and boost employment to further develop the country.
Increasing labour mobility	• The influence of MNCs on international trade has played a large role in the division of labour. • Manufacturing processes are now commonly outsourced to LIDCs to cut costs on production and labour • On the other hand, management roles and headquarters remain is ACs.

Case study – interdependence between trading partners

	Vietnam
Direction and components of current international trade patterns	• Major exports: electronics (smartphones, computers), textiles, footwear, seafood. • Key trading partners: China, USA, Japan, South Korea, EU. • Imports mainly include machinery, electronic components, and raw materials.
Changes in international trade patterns over time	• Shift from agriculture-based exports (rice, coffee) to manufacturing and technology sectors since the 2000s. • Integration into global supply chains, especially electronics and apparel industries. • Increasing participation in trade agreements (e.g. CPTPP, EVFTA) expanding market access.
Economic, political, social, and environmental interdependence	• Economic: dependence on foreign direct investment (FDI) and export markets for growth. • Political: trade agreements promote diplomatic ties; tensions exist over tariffs and regional influence. • Social: job creation in export industries improves incomes but can exacerbate urban-rural divides. • Environmental: rapid industrialisation linked to pollution and resource depletion; growing pressure for sustainable practices.
Impacts of trade on Vietnam	• Economic development: significant GDP growth, poverty reduction, rising middle class. • Political stability: economic success supports government legitimacy, but inequalities pose challenges. • Social equality: uneven benefits, with disparities between urban industrial zones and rural areas; labour rights concerns persist.

Global migration

Global migration flows and patterns

- **INTER-regional migration:** the movement of people between different regions (e.g. from Australia to the UK).
- **INTRA-regional migration:** the movement of people within the same region (e.g. moving from New York to Texas, or from Germany to Norway).
- Reasons for migration can be divided into two categories:
  - **Push factors:** the reasons for the motivation to leave the migrant's home country. Examples include persecution, unemployment, climate change, poor living standards.
  - **Pull factors:** reasons migrants are attracted to destination countries. Examples include political stability, education, and employment opportunities.
- **Inter-regional patterns of migration:**
  - Many people migrate due to conflict or economic strain. The Central Mediterranean route from Africa to Europe is one of the most common routes. This route is very dangerous, involving human trafficking and violence from smugglers – 2,800 deaths and disappearances occurred in 2022.
  - Migration from Asia to North America is also common, with around 14.6 million Asian immigrants living in the USA. Reasons mainly include better job prospects, higher living wage, and better advanced education opportunities.
  - Many sub-Saharan countries are also suffering from the impacts of climate change, causing migration to less vulnerable countries.
- **Intra-regional patterns of migration:**
  - Many migrants also travel from Eastern European countries to other EU members in West Europe as economic migrants. They often travel in search of better employment opportunities and higher wages, sending remittances back to their home country.
  - Migration back to home countries and family reunification is also common after people have obtained sufficient experience, education, or funds.

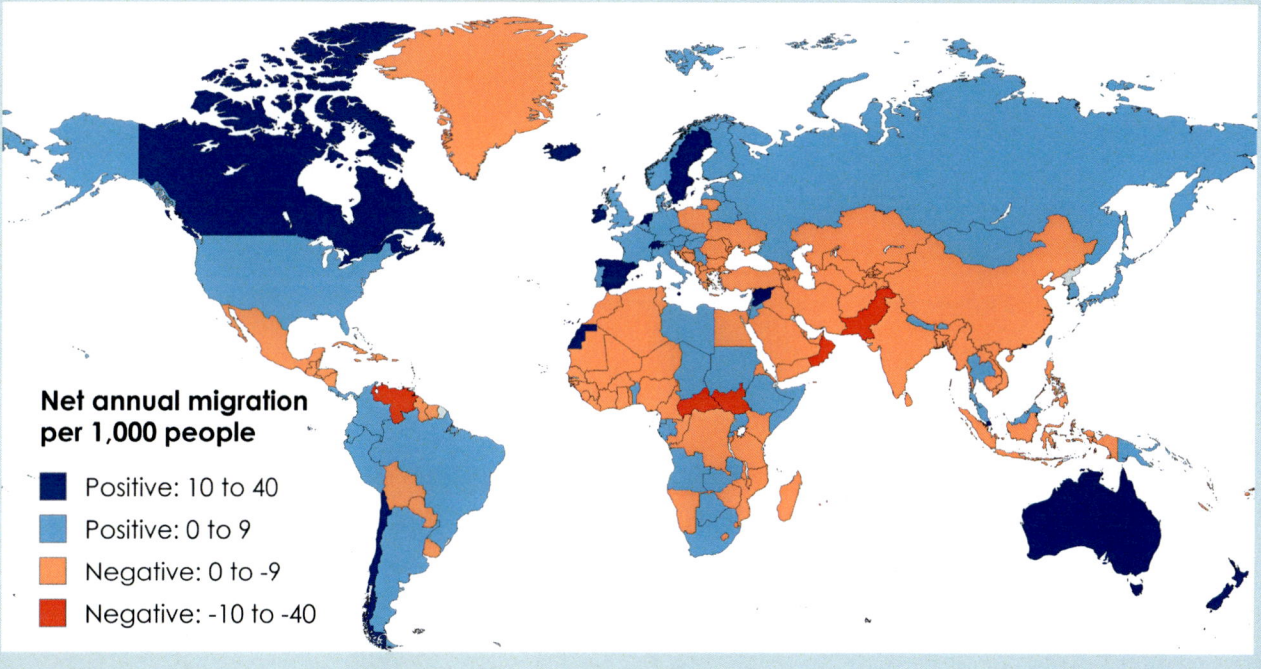

Net annual migration per 1,000 people
- Positive: 10 to 40
- Positive: 0 to 9
- Negative: 0 to -9
- Negative: -10 to -40

Global patterns of migration are interrelated and contribute to socio-economic development on an international scale. Two indicators can be used:
- **Migrant remittances:** money sent from migrants back to their country of origin, usually to financially support their family or community.
- **HDI:** Human Development Index. An index used to rank countries (0-1) in relation to their level of human development based on health (life expectancy), education and income.

One way socio-economic development is linked to migration can be seen through the relationship between remittances and a country's GDP. If a high proportion of their GDP is sourced from remittances sent back by emigrants of that country, this indicates weakness in the economy. For example:
- **High % of GDP from remittances:** limited local jobs and economic opportunities → people feel forced to migrate to earn money abroad → earnings are sent home as remittances → households rely on remittances rather than the internal economy → correlates to a lower HDI (e.g. Tajikistan: 51% of GDP is remittances; HDI is 0.691).
- **Low % of GDP from remittances:** strong local economy and prosperous job market → people rely on the money they make rather than remittances → less dependence on external sources of income → correlates with a higher HDI (e.g. Sweden: 0.6% of GDP is remittances; HDI is 0.952).

Global migration

Factors influencing global migration patterns

- **Economic globalisation:**
  - More migration within groups such as ASEAN due to better flow of remittances and ease of return if necessary.
  - Bilateral corridors such as Spain and Romania are increasingly popular
  - Growth in international trade and investment creates more demand for foreign labour in manufacturing, services, and tech sectors.
  - Expansion of multinational corporations encourages the movement of skilled and semi-skilled workers to meet global operational needs.
- **High concentration of young workers and female migrants:**
  - More younger people are migrating in search of better economic opportunities and job prospects than what is offered in their home country.
  - Female migrant workers now make up 38.7% of all migrant workers, many migrating from less developed countries or those where women still face job discrimination to gain more financial freedom and independence.
  - Many young migrants also seek educational opportunities abroad, often remaining in the host country to work after graduation.
  - Women are increasingly employed in healthcare, domestic work, and service industries, sometimes filling labour shortages in ageing societies.
- **South-South migration corridors:**
  - Migration through south-south corridors is now equal in size to south-north corridors.
  - Growing regional integration initiatives in Africa, Asia, and Latin America have reduced barriers to intra-regional movement.
  - Many South-South migrants move to neighbouring countries with similar languages and cultural norms, making adaptation easier.
- **Increased number of refugees:**
  - The number of refugees worldwide has increased by 7% to 43.4 million in 2023. The most refugees were from Afghanistan and Syria.
  - 69% of refugees are hosted in neighbouring countries, many with the intention of returning to their home countries.
  - This increase may be due to rising conflicts or political persecution. Climate-related disasters, such as floods and droughts, are increasingly forcing people to flee their home countries.
- **Changes in migration policies:**
  - Migration policies are created individually by countries to meet specific requirements.
  - For example, Singapore introduced a points-based system for immigration in 2023 (COMPASS) in which high earning and skilled individuals that score 40 points are granted an employment pass to live and work there.
  - Some countries have tightened visa requirements to protect domestic labour markets during economic downturns. Others have introduced fast-track systems for migrants with in-demand skills, such as IT specialists, healthcare professionals, and engineers.

Effects of global migration

Positive effects		
Stability	**Growth**	**Development**
• Migrants can send remittances back to their home country. This supports poorer families and helps to reduce poverty and reduce economic stress. • Returning migrants bring back new skills and knowledge.	• Migrants help to reduce pressure on industries that are experiences labour shortages such as healthcare and agriculture. • Migrants support the local economy of their destination country by spending their wages and through taxation. • Many may start new businesses, creating more jobs and stimulating the economy	• Remittances can help to improve standards of living by funding better healthcare, education and housing. • Returning migrants can use skills and experience in tech industries to develop their home countries and public services. • Migration helps to strengthen connections between countries, influencing factors like trade and peace-making.

Negative effects		
Inequalities	**Conflicts**	**Injustices**
• Skilled and educated workers often migrate, causing a 'brain drain' in the country of origin. • Remittances are only received by families with members living abroad, causing inequalities between those and others who don't receive the same support. • Migration of majority young, educated people means countries struggle to support their own economies and labour markets.	• Migration can cause political dispute, with some anti-immigration groups being formed, claiming immigration is a threat to national identity. • Migration may cause overpopulation in some areas, putting strain on public services like healthcare and schools. • Conflict can also occur at borders if migration isn't legal.	• Many migrants are falsely promised a better life abroad by traffickers but end up in exploitative conditions and put into forced labour. • Many refugees and asylum seekers live in poor conditions in detention centres and refugee camps.

Global migration

Case study – migration corridors

	Poland – UK corridor
Emigration patterns (people leaving Poland)	• Poland has experienced high rates of emigration. • Most migrants are working age males in search of higher wages and better employment opportunities. • Popular destination countries include the UK or those in the EU like Germany. • Overall, net emigration from Poland is decreasing.
Immigration patterns (people entering Poland)	• Most of Poland's immigrants come from neighbouring Eastern European countries, particularly Ukraine because of increased instability due to the war. • Many migrants are attracted to recent economic growth and labour shortages. • As of 2024 there were 1.13 million registered migrants in Poland, 2/3 are from Ukraine. • Overall, net immigration to Poland is increasing.
Impacts of migration from Poland to UK	**Economic:** • Polish immigrants can send migrant remittances back to their home country, supporting their communities and boosting the economy. • In the first quarter of 2025 alone, Poland received a total of €681 million in remittances. • On the other hand, the UK benefits from additional workforces, particularly in construction, healthcare and agriculture where there are labour shortages. This has helped to increase economic productivity. **Political:** • The migration corridor between the UK and Poland has improved relations between the countries. • Since the UK left the EU, increasing tension has occurred between some UK citizens and Polish migrants. • Brexit has also caused uncertainty for Polish people wanting to migrate to the UK as movement between the countries becomes more difficult. **Social:** • Large communities of Polish people have formed in cities such as Birmingham, Manchester, and London. • Right-wing political groups stoke racial tensions by arguing that immigrants harm national identity and reduce opportunities for British people.

Case study – opportunities and challenges of migration

	UK	Laos
Emigration patterns	• In 2024, 513,000 people emigrated from the UK. Common destination countries include Australia, New Zealand, Canada and the USA. • Most emigration occurs for work, education or retirement.	• In 2020, 1.3 million Laotians lived outside of Laos. • Emigration is mainly motivated by job seeking and searching for better employment opportunities.
Immigration patterns	• The UK has experienced net immigration with migrants from countries such as Poland, Romania, India and Nigeria. • In 2024, net migration was 431,000. • The main reasons for immigration are for education, asylum seeking and job opportunities.	• Immigration to Laos is minimal and mainly comprises of return migrants. • Some migrants arrive from neighbouring countries China and Vietnam.
Immigration policy	• Since leaving the EU, the UK has developed a points-based system, with a minimum of 70 points required to be eligible for approval. • These points can be gained based on salary, job offers, proficiency in the English language and education in STEM subjects.	• The Laos-Thailand migration corridor is a major flow of migrants from Laos, especially of those who are unskilled. • Trafficking policies have been put in place to protect vulnerable migrants from exploitation.
Opportunities from immigration	• Immigration to the UK helps to reduce labour shortages in important industries such as construction, healthcare, and agriculture. • Migrants also support the economy through tax paying, supporting public services and spending income. • Many migrants are working age which helps in reducing the strain of the aging population of the UK.	• Returning migrants bring skills and knowledge that can help to improve industry and development in Laos. • 15% of Laos households receive remittances, showing the country's reliance on migrants. This helps to support communities and increase standard of living.
Challenges from immigration	• Illegal immigration can cause conflict at borders and put strain on the UK's housing and public services. • Immigrants who have trouble integrating and building a new life in the UK may feel alienated or unwelcome, especially in areas with high anti-immigration sentiments.	• Human trafficking is a big issue for migrants with young people being targeted. • High emigration rates have negative impacts on Laos through a loss of labour force and brain drain. This can stunt the development of Laos.

Power and borders

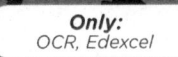 

Only: OCR, Edexcel

Sovereign nation states

Key definitions in understanding powers and borders:

- **State:** an independent area within a country with defined territory, government, sovereignty and permanent population
- **Nation:** a group or community of people that share culture, history, language, and identity. A nation is not always within one country and do not have sovereignty. For example, Kurdistan is a nation spread across the states of Iraq, Iran, Turkey, and Syria forming their own cultural identity and want for independence.
- **Sovereignty:** the supreme authority that states have enabling them to govern themselves. Internal sovereignty refers to the ability of a state to govern its own borders, external sovereignty refers to the ability to also involve with international affairs.
- **Territorial integrity:** the right of a state to defend its borders from external threat, whilst discouraging the use of force.
- **Norms:** the accepted standards and behaviours that society deems as acceptable. The United Nations Charter promotes the norm of peace between member states and the internal protection within them.
- **Intervention:** can take place when the human rights of individuals within a country are not protected. This may be due to war or persecution. Interventions can be through humanitarian support, military, economic (including sanctions against states) or involving organisations such as NATO.
- **Geopolitics:** the geopolitical power of states and countries varies across the world. Some countries have much more political power compared to others, such as the USA or China which are considered 'superpowers'.

Factors challenging sovereignty and territorial integrity

Erosion of sovereignty and loss of territorial integrity are influences by:

- **Current political boundaries:**
  - Separatism is when different types of groups within a larger region seek independence (e.g. the Basque Nation).
  - Historical disputes over rightful land ownership can cause conflict over borders. This may be due to availability of valuable resources or when ethnic boundaries misalign with political borders.
- **Transnational corporations (TNCs):**
  - Large TNCs often operate across many countries, including LIDCs who become reliant on the economic support and investment.
  - As a result, TNCs develop political and economic power that can often override that of the government, influencing national policies and allowing them to exploit their resources and labour market.
- **Supranational institutions:**
  - In order to have membership to a supranational body such as the EU or ASEAN, member states are required to compromise some sovereignty for the collective goals of the group (for example free trade).
  - Tensions arise when national interests conflict with supranational goals. For example, the EU requires all member states to uphold common policies. This can partly explain the reasoning for Brexit as some people believed the EU threatened the sovereignty of the UK.
- **Political dominance of ethnic groups:**
  - Some countries are home to many ethnic groups. This can lead to tensions regarding their independence and possible creation of new states which threatens territorial integrity.
  - Different ethnic groups also raises issues with how the country should be run and who should represent the people, leading to conflicting opinions on political decisions.

Case study – challenges to sovereignty

	Syria humanitarian crisis
Causes and challenges to government sovereignty	• Civil war triggered by 2011 Arab Spring protests against authoritarian rule. • Authoritarian legacy under Assad entrenched corruption, repression, and sectarianism • Foreign intervention from Turkey, Iran, USA, and Gulf states fuels fragmentation. • Post-Assad instability: regime collapsed Dec 2024; interim government under Ahmed al-Sharaa lacks legitimacy and multiple armed groups resist integration. • Constitutional disputes between Kurds, Druze, and Alawites. • Economic collapse: hyperinflation, sanctions, infrastructure destruction block recovery.
Impacts on people and places	• 16.7 million people in need of aid; 12 million people displaced; 4.2 million refugees. • Mass casualties and trauma from sectarian violence. • Minority exclusion drives unrest and protests. • Infrastructure loss – dam attacks and urban destruction cause power and water shortages. • Blockades and aid barriers limit humanitarian relief. • Economic stagnation: GDP growth is only ~1.3% (would take decades to recover to 2010 levels). • Justice gap: limited progress on transitional justice and missing persons. • External actors (Turkey, Israel, USA, Jordan) shape outcomes, limiting sovereignty.

Power and borders

Only: OCR, Edexcel

Global governance and responding to conflict
- **What causes conflict?**
  - Divisions between ethnic or religious groups
  - Corruption within the government or a lack of protection over its citizens
  - Competition for limited resources such as water or oil
  - Persecution of groups based on religion or political standing.
- For example, the Nile River flows through 11 countries and is the primary freshwater source for many countries. Conflict has occurred over the shared water access, with Egypt, Ethiopia and Sudan exerting most power.
  - The construction of the Grand Ethiopian Renaissance Dam began in the aim of generating large amounts of hydroelectric power for Ethiopia, however Egypt claims that the dam will dramatically reduce downstream water availability, threatening public safety.
  - Disputes are currently unresolved, and negotiations have not been made so tensions remain.

Resolving conflicts	
Institutions	• UN is responsible for overseeing peacekeeping missions, sanctions and conflicts. They aim to promote human rights, build relations between nations and maintain international law. For example, the UN Mission in the Republic of South Sudan (UNMISS) • NATO is an alliance with 32 members that aim to safeguard their freedom and security using political and military means. One example of an operation and intervention by NATO was to protect the civilians of Kosovo in 1999.
Treaties	• Treaties are international agreements, often established through institutions like the UN. They aim to uphold principles of sovereignty and peaceful conflict resolution.
Laws	• International humanitarian laws are in place to protect populations from the impacts of political disputes and conflicts. Breaches of this law are taken to the International Crime Court.
Norms	• Norms are common practices outlined in the UN Charter which help in forming agreements, treaties and laws.

- **Geopolitical intervention:**
  - Advancing technology (such as drones) has increased the ability of surveillance and monitoring of peacekeeping to ensure humanitarian laws are respected.
  - During conflict, many refuges flee areas that are unsafe in search of asylum.
  - In response, workers of NGOs and enter these conflict zones to provide care, aid and financial support.
  - To successfully transfer this support, flows of ideas are required.

Global to local cooperation
Case Study: South Sudan conflict
- **Interventions and interactions of organisations:**
  - **United Nations:** UNMISS peacekeeping mission to protect civilians and support peace processes.
  - **National government:** South Sudanese government involved in ceasefire negotiations and rebuilding efforts.
  - **NGOs:** Médecins Sans Frontières (MSF) and others provide humanitarian aid, medical care, and support displaced people.
- **Consequences of global governance for local communities:**
  - Improved protection and delivery of aid, reducing immediate suffering.
  - Some progress towards political stability, but intermittent violence continues.
  - Displacement and trauma remain significant; rebuilding social trust is ongoing.
  - Challenges include limited access to remote areas and dependence on aid.

Global governance of sovereignty and territorial integrity

	Global governance of sovereignty issues	Global governance of territorial integrity
Short term effects	• Humanitarian aid is a response to conflicts, disasters, famine or persecution in the form of protecting civilians by providing food, healthcare and shelter. • Refugees and displaced individuals are supported	• Peacekeeping forces and aid help to protect populations at risk by reducing violence and assisting displaced individuals. • Human rights violations are monitored. • Improved border control to facilitate trade and flow of goods and services.
Long term effects	• Intervention and pressure from external governors can lead to democratic reform and transition of politics in a country. Many countries are provided with support in developing a fairer government and electoral process. • Countries can easily become dependent on aid, so programmes have been put in place to reduce this reliance through improving food security, housing and sanitation.	• Improving trade relationships to foster new economic and investment opportunities. • Support for fair elections and legal reform to regain state authority. • Reclamation and restoration of territory.

Health and disease

All specs except: Edexcel, WJEC, Eduqas

Classification and patterns of disease
- **Infectious:** diseases spread by pathogens like bacteria, fungi or virus (e.g. HIV).
- **Non-infectious:** diseases not caused by pathogens that can't be spread (e.g. heart disease).
- **Communicable:** diseases that can be spread directly or indirectly between individuals (e.g. influenza).
- **Non-communicable:** diseases that can't be spread between people (e.g. lung cancer).
- **Contagious:** diseases that are spread through direct contact (e.g. chickenpox).
- **Non-contagious:** diseases that require an alternate mode of transmission, such as water or a vector – an organism that transmits the pathogen (e.g. malaria).
- **Epidemic:** when an outbreak of disease occurs in a specific area and affects many people.
- **Endemic:** the consistent presence of a disease in a particular area. For example, malaria is an endemic in several African countries.
- **Pandemic:** when a disease has spread worldwide across multiple countries (e.g. the COVID-19 pandemic or the bubonic plague in the 14th century).
- **Zoonotic diseases:** can be passed between animals and humans. These diseases are more common when access to animal vaccinations is limited, animals live in close proximity to/within urban areas, or stray animals are common.

Disease	Global distribution
Malaria	An infectious but non-contagious disease, spread by mosquitos as vectors. In 2023, there were approximately 263 million cases of malaria worldwide, 94% of which were in Africa. Over half of all malaria caused deaths were in Nigeria, the Democratic Republic of the Congo, Niger and Tanzania.
HIV	An infectious and communicable disease spread through direct contact. In 2023, there were 39.9 million people living with HIV. African countries are most affected, accounting for 2/3 people with HIV.
Tuberculosis	An infectious airborne disease. In 2023, approximately 10.8 million people had TB and 1.25 million died. Most cases occurred in South-East Asia and Africa.
Diabetes	A non-infectious and non-communicable disease linked to lifestyle and obesity. In 2022, 830 million people suffered with diabetes. Most cases are type 2 diabetes which are often preventable. Cases are prevalent in Asia and the USA.
Cardio-vascular disease	A non-infectious and non-communicable disease, also linked to lifestyle. In 2019, 17.9 million people died due to CVD. Cases are common in most parts of the world, however over 75% of deaths occurred in low or middle income countries. This may be due to lack of sufficient healthcare or economic stability.

- There are four main types of disease diffusion:
  - **Expansion:** when disease spreads outwards from its source location, whilst maintaining high amounts of cases at the source.
  - **Relocation:** when diseases move from one location to another, often due to travelling or migration.
  - **Contagious:** spread via direct contact between infected people.
  - **Hierarchical:** when disease spreads via an ordered sequence such as from larger cities to smaller towns via transport links.
- **Physical barriers to diffusion:** mountain ranges, oceans, deserts, harsh climate or those that are unsuitable for certain diseases.
- **Socio-economic barriers to diffusion:** vaccinations, quarantines or isolations.

Factors affecting the prevalence of disease
- **Temperature:** many diseases require warm and humid climates to survive and be transmitted. High altitude regions are colder so less prone to vectors and waterborne diseases.
- **Rainfall:** wet regions that experience high rainfall means there is more water bodies for vectors to grow (e.g. mosquitoes around stagnant water). On the other hand, droughts can cause sanitation issues leading to water borne diseases like cholera.
- **Seasons:** some pathogens survive better in certain climates meaning outbreaks are more severe at certain times of year.
- **Climate change:** increasing temperatures due to global warming means vectors can survive for longer and in more areas (higher and lower latitudes). Climate change can also bring more humidity and rainfall as excess moisture can be held in warmer air and more water vapour in the atmosphere as evaporation increases. These conditions are ideal for vectors (e.g. ticks carrying Lyme disease surviving for longer as winters become milder in Europe).

Case study – natural hazards affecting disease spread

	Haiti Earthquake (2010) and cholera outbreak
Geographical area	• Earthquake struck Port-au-Prince and surrounding regions, devastating infrastructure. • Disrupted water and sanitation systems increased vulnerability to cholera outbreak.
Environment factors affecting spread	• Tropical climate with rainy seasons facilitated waterborne disease transmission. • Contaminated water sources and poor sanitation worsened spread.
Human factors affecting spread	• High population density in temporary camps increased transmission rates. • Limited access to clean water and healthcare. • Low immunisation coverage against cholera before outbreak.
Impacts on populations	• Over 800,000 cholera cases and 10,000 deaths. • Strain on health services and social disruption.
Strategies to minimise impacts	• National: Emergency water sanitation programs, oral cholera vaccination campaigns. • International: Support from WHO, MSF, and NGOs for treatment centres and education. • Long-term efforts to improve water infrastructure and hygiene education.

Health and disease

All specs except: Edexcel, WJEC, Eduqas

Trends in communicable and non-communicable diseases

Rising living standards in a country reduces communicable diseases. As infrastructure and sanitation improves, and availability of clean water increases, cases of waterborne diseases like cholera fall. Furthermore, access to healthcare provides people with vaccinations which can prevent outbreaks and reduce mortality rates.

The epidemiological transition model:
- **Stage 1:** high mortality from infectious diseases, famine, and poor sanitation. This was typical of pre-industrial societies when life expectancy was ~20–40 years.
- **Stage 2:** improvements in sanitation and medicine from industrialisation lowers mortality and raises life expectancy.
- **Stage 3:** chronic diseases overtake infectious ones as lifestyle factors impact health.
- **Stage 4:** advanced healthcare prevents illness; mortality concentrated in older ages.
- **Stage 5:** possible re-emergence of infectious diseases due to climate change, antibiotic resistance, new pathogens, globalisation, etc.

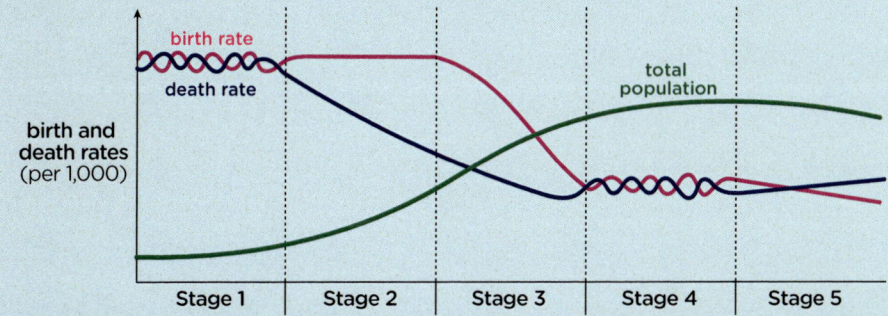

Why is there more communicable disease in LIDCs?	Why is there more non-communicable disease in ACs?
• Poor water and sanitation in less developed countries means waterborne diseases are much more likely to spread. Cholera and polio are common in some poorer African countries compared to ACs where cases are extremely rare. • Inadequate healthcare means vaccinations are less available and outbreaks are more difficult to control. • Undernourishment due to insufficient access to food weakens immune systems, making people more susceptible to disease. • Despite this, noncommunicable diseases relating to poor nutrition also exist.	• Populations in advanced countries have much more sedentary lifestyles (due to office jobs etc.). • Overconsumption of high calorie foods is linked to high levels of type 2 diabetes, cardiovascular diseases and obesity related illnesses. • Lifestyle choices such as smoking and alcohol consumption also correlate to cancer cases. • Communicable diseases are still very common, however advancing technology, medicine, and healthcare access means the spread of many diseases is reduced.

Case study – disease causes and response strategies

	Communicable disease: malaria in Nigeria	Non-communicable disease: CVD in the UK
Environmental and human causes	• Warm, humid climate and abundant standing water provide ideal mosquito breeding grounds. • Poor sanitation, inadequate housing, and limited access to healthcare increase transmission.	• High prevalence linked to sedentary lifestyle, poor diet, smoking, and alcohol use. • Socio-economic inequalities influence incidence rates.
Prevalence, incidence, and patterns	• Nigeria accounts for ~27% of global malaria cases. • High incidence in rural areas and during rainy seasons.	• CVD remains a leading cause of death, accounting for ~26% of all UK deaths annually. • Higher rates in deprived areas and older populations.
Socio-economic impacts	• High mortality, especially among children under five. • Economic burden from lost productivity and healthcare costs. • Strains healthcare systems and exacerbates poverty cycles.	• Significant healthcare costs and loss of productivity. • Impacts quality of life and life expectancy disparities.
Strategies to mitigate and respond	• Government-led distribution of insecticide-treated nets (ITNs) and indoor residual spraying. • International support via Global Fund, WHO, and NGOs for diagnosis, treatment, and education. • Community health worker programs to improve access in remote areas.	• Public health campaigns promoting healthy lifestyle changes. • NHS screening and treatment programs, including cholesterol management and smoking cessation. • Policy measures such as sugar taxes and regulations on advertising unhealthy foods.

Health and disease

All specs except: Edexcel, WJEC, Eduqas

Increasing global mobility affecting diffusion of disease
- **The World Health Organisation (WHO):** an international organisation with 194 member states. WHO facilitates research into disease, gathering data from each member with the aim of supporting countries with disease outbreaks (e.g. via vaccination programmes).
- **The outbreak of H1N1:**
  - April 2009: the H1N1 influenza virus strain was first detected in North America, leading the USA to declare a public health emergency.
  - June 2009: the WHO declared the H1N1 a pandemic. 74 countries had confirmed infections.
  - August 2010: cases had declined and the WHO declared the end of the H1N1 pandemic.
  - It was estimated that there were over 60 million cases and 12,000 deaths, however these numbers may be much higher.

Physical barriers affecting mitigation and responses	
Relief	Mountain ranges and harsh environments can make it difficult for aid providers and healthcare services to access infected people. However, these barriers may reduce transmission.
Natural hazards	Disasters such as earthquakes can also prevent access of healthcare workers and medicine provision. They can also cause the spread of diseases if infrastructure is damaged and sanitation is poor.
Excess water	Floods can spread waterborne diseases much faster. They also limit access of supplies and aid.
Remote communities	In rural regions, healthcare is often poor and access for vaccinations and treatment is difficult.

- **HIV (Human Immunodeficiency Virus)** is a disease that attacks the body's immune system, transmitted through direct contact (unprotected sex, needle sharing, blood transfusions, from mother to child). HIV can develop into AIDS, the late stage of the disease where it is extremely hard for the body to fight infection.

Mitigation strategies for HIV/AIDS	
Screening	Early diagnosis of HIV can limit its development into AIDS meaning treatment can be provided and reduce the risk of transmission.
Education	Educational programmes to spread awareness of how the disease is transmitted so that people can practice safe sex and understand the risk of sharing needles for drug use.
Funding of treatment	Antiretroviral therapy (ART) is a treatment method for HIV that involves multiple medications to make the virus undetectable, allow recovery of the immune system and preventing it from being transmissible.

Nature as a source of medicines
- Nature is a source of medicine and has been used by humans to treat conditions and diseases throughout history.
  - **Morphine:** an opioid drug, used as a powerful painkiller in medicinal treatment. Morphine is derived from opium poppy seeds, grown in warm climates. Commonly in Asian and Middle Eastern countries. It requires fertile loam or sand soils that are well drained.
  - **Salicin:** an anti-inflammatory and pain-relieving drug derived from the bark of willow trees. It requires temperate climates with sufficient rainfall, commonly found in wet areas, and grows best in well-drained soil that is slightly acidic.
  - **Rosy periwinkle:** extracts used globally in pharmaceuticals to treat leukaemia and Hodgkin's lymphoma. Its trade is regulated due to conservation concerns and intellectual property rights. It is native to Madagascar and thrives in tropical, subtropical climates with well-drained soils and moderate rainfall. However, its overharvesting threatens wild populations, so cultivation programs promote sustainability, habitat protection, and propagation research, with benefit-sharing agreements to ensure local communities gain economically.
- **Conservation issues:** many medicinal plants are now endangered species due to overharvesting. Habitat loss from deforestation has also destroyed the environment of which many plants grow.

Strategies for disease risk and eradication
- **Global campaign for disease eradication – Polio:**
  - The Global Polio Eradication Initiative (GPEI) began in 1988 with the goal to eradicate polio using the oral polio vaccine (OPV), surveillance systems to monitor outbreaks.
  - Since its launch, there has been a 99% decrease in polio cases.
  - The campaign was mostly successful; however, Polio is still endemic in Afghanistan and Pakistan due to challenges faced because of conflicts and political unrest.
- **National campaign for disease eradication – Malaria:**
  - The National Malaria Elimination Strategic Plan (NMESP) developed in 2017 in the aim of eliminating cases of Malaria which is endemic in Zambia.
  - Working with WHO and other organisations, the objective is to distribute insect nets, rapid testing and strengthen surveillance.
  - Bottom-up strategies are often more welcome in communities:
  - Women in communities are often not involved in the eradication of disease.
  - In rural areas, women are often who manages water, food and hygiene practices. Therefore, educating women in how do reduce waterborne and sanitation diseases whilst providing medications and vaccinations to all could help to decrease diseases and eradicate them in the future.

Food security

All specs except: Edexcel, CIE

Variations in patterns of food security
- According to the UN Food and Agriculture Organisation (FAO):

  "Food security exists when all people, at all times, have physical and economic access to sufficient, safe and nutritious food that meets their dietary needs and food preferences for an active and healthy life"
- There are three pillars of food security:
  - **Availability:** the quantity of food in the supply chain, including production levels, stock, and trading activity.
  - **Access:** individuals have sufficient means of acquiring food. This relies on factors like income, fertile/arable land, and safe transport routes.
  - **Utilisation:** food must provide the body with the nutrients and energy needed to live healthily. This includes good sanitation and high quality food.
- The stability of these pillars is heavily interconnected, with the failure of one often having knock-on effects on the general food security of an area or population.
- Within and between countries, many inequalities influence food security, such as:
  - Western provinces of China including Tibet, Gansu, and Yunnan experience poorer food security than wealthier Eastern provinces like Shanghai and Beijing.
  - Northern African countries such as Morocco, Algeria, and Tunisia have lower levels of hunger compared to Chad, South Sudan, and Central African Republic. This can be attributed to stark differences in several factors including political instability, climate, and quality of infrastructure.
- The **Global Food Security Index** for 2022 identifies patterns in recent global food security. The table below highlights the top and bottom five countries globally, calculated based on the affordability, availability, quality and safety of their food on a scale of 0–100. Higher scores indicate higher levels of food security.

Top 5 countries (2022)	Rating	Bottom 5 countries (2022)	Rating
Finland	83.7	Syria	36.3
Ireland	81.7	Haiti	38.5
Norway	80.5	Yemen	40.1
France	80.2	Sierra Leone	40.5
Netherlands	80.1	Madagascar	40.6

- The **Global Hunger Index** also helps us to understand patterns of food security, calculating scores for each country using a scale of 0–100. It considers four factors:
  - **Undernourishment:** not reaching sufficient calorific intake.
  - **Child stunting:** proportion of children with low height for their age.
  - **Child wasting:** proportion of children with low weight for their age.
  - **Child mortality:** death rate of children under the age of 5.
- In 2024, all countries ranked as having alarming levels of hunger (35.0–49.9) were in Africa: Madagascar, Chad, Yemen, Somalia, Burundi, and South Sudan. Most of the rest of Africa experiences serious levels (20.0–34.9), as do several countries in Asia including India, Pakistan, and Afghanistan.

Theoretical positions on food security
- **Malthusian Theory** (Thomas Malthus in 1798): argues that populations increase exponentially (e.g. 2, 4, 8, 16, 32, etc.) whereas food supply increases arithmetically (e.g. 1, 2, 3, 4, 5, etc.) meaning populations will outgrow the available food supply. This can only be controlled by limiting population growth or through 'natural checks' such as disease which brings population back to a manageable level.
- **Boserupian Theory** (Ester Boserup in 1965): argues that the need for more food as population increases will foster innovation in food production. Methods such as genetic modification and advancing machinery have been developed to produce more food and reduce insecurities.

Global food production system
The production of food relies on certain conditions of air, climate, soil, and water.
- **Air:** plants require CO_2 from the atmosphere to photosynthesise using light energy to produce glucose needed for energy. Some plants convert atmospheric nitrogen into molecules essential for growth. Poor air quality can stunt plant growth, reduce their health and hinder photosynthesis.
- **Climate:** plants grow within optimum temperature ranges. Some crops rely on seasonal patterns (e.g. rice paddies in monsoon seasons). Rainfall, droughts, flooding, and too much/little sunlight can severely impact or even destroy crops.
- **Soil:** different soil types (sand, silt, clay, loam) have different properties that impact growth of different plants. Slightly acidic soils are optimal for most plants, whereas overcultivation strips nutrients and reduces productivity.
- **Water:** is an essential solvent in the process of photosynthesis and in transpiration of nutrients. Different methods of irrigation can be used to better supply water to plants. Water scarcity can severely stunt plant growth.

Feeding the world's population
Food production process:
- **Initial food production:** includes growing/farming/harvesting crops, fishing, and rearing livestock, as well as processing, packaging, and storing raw materials.
- **Transportation:** food often travels long distances by air, sea, rail, and road before reaching the consumer. This distance is known as 'food miles.'
- **Consumption:** food is eaten by consumers. Overconsumption is an increasing issue in developed countries, leading to rising obesity and food wastage.

Food production methods:
- **Intensive farming:** high input of labour/money = high output (e.g. cattle in the USA).
- **Extensive farming:** large scale farming where inputs and outputs are low, often consisting of basic farming techniques on large areas of land (e.g. sheep in Wales)
- **Subsistence farming:** small scale farming that provides for a single household or community; often traditional methods that are labour-intensive (e.g. rice in China).
- **Commercial farming:** farming with the intention of selling produce for profit. This can form large scale agribusinesses that use high inputs of technology and capital to produce high output (e.g. wheat).

Food security

Effects of globalisation on the food industry

- **Globalisation** refers to the world's increasing interconnectedness between countries through trade, technology, travel and the interactions between cultures and sharing of ideas. As countries become more integrated into the global economy, many see economic development and higher disposable incomes within families. This allows for the consumption of more processed and imported foods.
- Globalisation helps meet the food demands of the increasing global population: countries can easily import food and TNCs can support food supply.
- Greater exposure to new foods and cuisines through media, migration and tourism causes a shift in people's tastes (e.g. demand for Indian cuisine in the UK).
- **Issues caused by globalisation of the food industry:**
    - **Food miles:** refers to the distance food travels from producer to consumer. Due to globalisation, changing demands mean food miles have increased. Longer supply chains mean there are more greenhouse gas (GHG) emissions from transport. For example, pineapple imports from Costa Rica to the UK travel around 5,424 miles.
    - **Inequality between TNCs and small suppliers:** the increasingly powerful role of transnational corporations such as Unilever and Nestle has damaging effects on local suppliers. They often receive a very small percentage of profits made by these TNCs. Organisations such as Fairtrade aim to tackle this issue by ensuring producers get a certain price for their goods.
    - **Obesity:** the shift from traditional diets towards unhealthy processed foods has caused an increase in obesity and related illnesses. Globalisation through fast food chains and advertising has exacerbated this issue.
    - **Price crisis:** increased interconnectedness of the food industry means it is very vulnerable to the effects of politics (e.g. wars), climate change (e.g. droughts, natural disasters) and economic issues (e.g. 2008 GFC, COVID-19). As food travels further, a disruption in one region affects its global price because of a limited supply but high demand. For example, in 2022 the Russo-Ukraine War majorly disrupted grain exports causing global spikes in wheat prices
- **Opportunities created by globalisation of the food industry:**
    - **Technological innovation:** as knowledge, research and technology is shared across the world, the food industry benefits from rapid technological innovation. For example, genetic modification (GM) is a technique developed to alter the genetic makeup of plant species to enhance traits such as increased yield, pest resistance and tolerance to harsh climates. Another example is vertical farming methods in countries like Japan to grow food and maximise land use.
    - **Short-term food relief:** international trading relationships allow food to be imported across borders. Aid can be supplied with the help of organisations such as UN to countries in need after natural disasters or during conflicts to help prevent famine and malnutrition during these emergencies.
    - **Consumer choice:** globalisation has allowed consumer's access to a much broader range of foods, with imports from worldwide being available all year round. With increased interconnectedness influencing food preferences, hundreds of cuisines are available in restaurants and supermarkets.

Factors influencing food security

	Factor	Influence on food security
Physical factors	Geology	Rock types and their composition determines the formation of soil which affects food growth. Hard rocky ground limits root growth and water absorption.
	Soil	Fertile soils enable higher yields of crops. Overcultivation of soil reduces its fertility and limits food production. Loam soil is favoured for agriculture.
	Length of growing season	Different crops require growing seasons of different lengths. This can be influenced by climate and poor conditions can cause crop failure.
	Water availability	Crops must have their water demands met to grow well. Crops such as rice need to be well irrigated, and livestock also need drinking water.
	Slope	Very few crops can grow well on steep slopes. Water runoff can cause soil erosion and washing away of nutrients and moisture. Terracing the land can prevent erosion and surface runoff.
Social, economic, and political factors	Land ownership and capital	Landowners usually determine the distribution and production of food which affects food security. Ownerships can include owner-occupiers, tenants or landless labourers. In advanced countries, farming is capital intensive whereas in low income developing countries capital can be limited, leading to vulnerability to food insecurity.
	Technology	Access to modern technology can help to increase crop yield such as by maximising land, advanced machinery and improving pest resistance. However, advanced and wealthier regions are more able to access this technology whereas less developed countries often rely on traditional methods.
	Competition	As urbanisation increases and populations grow, the demand for land also increases. As a result, less land is available for food production and agriculture, causing costs of land to increase often pricing out local farmers. The growing dominance of TNCs and agribusinesses also damages the business of small, local farmers.
	Land grabbing	Refers to the legal or illegal acquisition of land on a large scale. Countries may land grab when food insecurity is an issue, so they use land elsewhere in which more water or fertile land is available. This can cause displacement of farmers and conflict as a result.

Food security

Risks to food security

In 2023, approximately 2.33 billion people worldwide experienced moderate or severe food insecurity. There are many social, political, environmental, and economic reasons as to why food insecurity exists, and these can form patterns that identify those most vulnerable.

- **LIDCs:** a lack of infrastructure and technology in many LIDCs means populations often lack the resources needed for sufficient food production and distribution. As a result, many rely on subsistence farming that is very volatile and vulnerable to shocks such as natural disasters and extreme weather.
- **Rural regions:** isolation of rural regions means there is limited access to the food supply chain. Difficult terrain and limited transport links also reduce food security.
- **Women and children:** women are often more food insecure than men. This impacts health during pregnancy and therefore infant and maternal mortality rates.
- **Areas affected by climate change:** regions impacted by droughts, floods and other extreme weather events can destroy crops and impact agricultural practices. This can be through limited water availability, desertification, or flooding of crops.
- **Conflict and political instability:** war and the displacement of people disrupts supply chains, destroys infrastructure, and limits the reach of aid. This means people's access to food is insufficient and food security worsens.
- **Pinch points:** in the food supply chain are locations where disruption can occur to the transportation, distribution or storage of food. Common pinch points are:
  - Damage or blockages to transport routes such as roads or ports. For example, the blockage of the Suez Canal in 2021 caused global delays.
  - Labour shortages or strikes can impact the distribution of food.
  - If perishable food is stored insufficiently (broken freezer or refrigerated facilities), large volumes of food can go to waste.
- **Food waste:** waste occurs at all stages of the food production chain:
  - Pests, diseases and extreme weather can cause rapid food loss at the growth stage.
  - Failure to meet quality control standards, poor storage or technical faults can cause waste at the processing stage.
  - Many food products fail to meet cosmetic supermarket standards.
  - According to the United Nations Food Waste Index Report in 2024, approximately 1 billion meals are wasted or lost every day, contributing to greenhouse gas emissions.
- **Desertification:** when land is continuously degraded due to climatic processes and human activity such as overcultivation. Desertification causes reduced soil fertility and vegetation loss. Countries can be increasingly reliant on aid as a form of food supply, and local farmers lose business and can no longer produce enough food.

Causes of desertification

Physical	Human
• Drought and insufficient rainfall. • High temperatures which increase evaporation of moisture from soils. • Wind erosion removes fertile soil. • Climate change enhances these causes.	• Overcultivation reduces soil fertility. • Overgrazing of livestock compacts the ground and removes vegetation. • Deforestation removes trees and vegetation that help to retain soil moisture.

Impacts on the food system

Event	Impact
Wildfires	Increasing global temperatures means many countries suffer from extremely hot periods. This causes land to become dry which increases vulnerability to and number of wildfires. As a result, farmland and crops are destroyed as well as infrastructure vital to food production.
El Nino	The enhanced effects of El Nino mean certain places such as Australia experience drought whereas others experience flooding.
Floods	Extreme weather events and intense rainfall means flooding occurs. This washes away layers of soil and waterlogs crops causing them to die.
Drought	Insufficient water supply and rainfall means crops fail due to poor irrigation. Livestock also suffer and can die as a result.
Water scarcity	Can be caused by climate change or over abstraction of water. This results in insufficient supply for irrigation systems, reduced crop yields, and increased competition for food causing price shocks.
Tectonic hazards	Earthquakes, volcanic eruptions, and tsunamis can damage critical elements of the food supply chain, resulting in the destruction of farmland, irrigation systems, warehouses, and factories, and the death of livestock. Damage to roads, railways and transport also means food cannot be distributed, and contamination of water supplies due to natural disasters can reduce water access and cause a lack of supply to irrigation systems.

Food security

All specs except: Edexcel, CIE

Imbalance in the global food system

Attempts to increase food security	Impacts on the physical environment
Irrigation and salinisation	Salination is common in arid/semi-arid regions as salt accumulates on the surface of soil, reducing soil fertility and plant life. Poor drainage and irrigation systems also mean that surface water evaporates quickly, leaving behind salt that was in the water. This can lead to desertification and reduced crop yield.
Deforestation	Forests are cleared for agricultural purposes and livestock grazing, causing a large decrease in biodiversity as vegetation is destroyed, habitats are lost, and animals die. A reduction in forest cover means surface runoff and soil erosion occurs which reduces soil fertility.
Changing landscapes	As populations grow and the need for food rises, more land is being converted to agricultural land. This involves replacing diverse woodland and other habitats with monoculture/single crop farms. Land is also adapted to make room for large agricultural machinery.
Water quality from agrochemicals	Agrochemicals include fertilisers, pesticides, insecticides and herbicides. When rain falls over soil treated with these chemicals, the surface runoff picks them up and flows into rivers, lakes or groundwater storage. This process is called eutrophication and can damage aquatic habitats by causing algal blooms and limiting the oxygen content of water, killing fish. These fish are then eaten by predators and drinking water is contaminated which has harmful effects on animals and humans.

Impact of issues related food insecurity on people
- **Food shortages:**
  - When people don't have sufficient access to enough healthy food and their calorie intake is not high enough, they can suffer from undernutrition and malnutrition.
  - In children, undernutrition can significantly stunt development and weaken the immune system.
  - A lack of certain vitamins and minerals can cause certain illnesses. For example, a lack of iron can cause anaemia, and a lack of vitamin C can cause scurvy.
- **Food surplus and poor diet:**
  - When people's calorie intake is above what is needed to maintain a healthy lifestyle, this is known as overnutrition.
  - Can cause obesity and illnesses such as type 2 diabetes, high blood pressure and cardiovascular diseases.
- **Increased use of chemicals and pesticides:**
  - When agrochemicals enter the food and water supply, there can be a risk to human health.
  - Digestion of these chemicals may be related to illnesses.

Food as a geopolitical commodity

Food can be classed as a geopolitical commodity because of how it is interconnected with trade, power, politics, and competition.

	Role in the global food system
Agribusiness	Conduct large-scale commercial farming for profit. They are often involved with food producers, manufacturers of machinery, chemical companies and other factors of the supply chain. One negative impact is that they often prioritise profit over the environment and local food needs.
TNCs	TNCs (e.g. Nestle, Unilever) operate on a global scale, often controlling sections of the food supply such as processing.
Food retailers	Retailers like Tesco and Sainsbury's play a big part in the global food system. They influence food prices and what is available to consumers. Globalisation has meant that large retailers have lots of control which creates a power imbalance with small suppliers.
Fair trade organisations	Aim to ensure farmers in LIDCs and EDCs receive fair payment for their produce and have safe working conditions.

- **Opportunities between countries to ensure food security:**
  - **Trading policies:** many countries are members of trade blocs and have trade agreements that allow for flow of food and agricultural products between members while charging tariffs to non-members.
  - **World Trade Organization:** the WTO acts as a platform for international trade discussions (e.g. creating fairer competition, reducing barriers on LIDCs).
  - **Aid:** food aid helps to support populations that suffer from food insecurity for multiple reasons such as conflict, climate crisis, poverty or natural disaster. Aid can also help to improve long term food security through improving agricultural practices, land and providing training.

Strategies to improve food security

Approaches to improving food security can be:
- **Long term:** strategies that aim to address underlying causes of food insecurity. For example, this may be through capacity building (training and education for improved agricultural techniques) or infrastructure development.
- **Short term:** strategies that aim to provide immediate relief to reduce food insecurity and prevent hunger. This is normally in the form of food aid distribution.
- **Large scale/top-down techniques:** tend to be able to support larger populations but will involve high energy usage and high initial costs (e.g. genetic modification).
- **Small scale/bottom-up techniques:** tend to be low cost and suitable for LIDCs and poorer communities, with fewer environmental impacts and more community resilience (e.g. sack gardening).

Human rights

Only: OCR, Edexcel

Global variation in human rights norms
The United Nations defines human rights as:

> "Rights inherent to all human beings, regardless of race, sex, nationality, ethnicity, language, religion or any other status ... Everyone is entitled to these rights, without discrimination."

There are 30 human rights, including the rights to be equal and recognised by the law, own a property, have freedom of opinion and the right to education.

Key terms for human rights:
- **Norms:** accepted standards and behaviours that society deems as 'normal' which often vary spatially and culturally. This means human rights are often interpreted differently in different countries because of religion and other influencing factors.
- **Intervention:** the use of military force by a country or organisation in foreign regions to protect the human rights of its people. This must be approved by the UN Security Council. Intervention does not always have to involve military force. NGOs and activists can also play a big role in intervening human rights violations.
- **Geopolitics:** the role of geography, economics and politics plays in international relations. A country's power to intervene in human rights issues and the consequence of doing so is heavily interrelated with geopolitics.

Factors influencing patterns of human rights violations

Forced labour	Maternal mortality rates	Capital punishment
When people are required to work by an employer under the threat of violence or other harmful consequences. Patterns: <ul><li>Affects 27.6 million people worldwide.</li><li>Predominantly occurs in Asia, Middle East and the Pacific region.</li><li>Heavily linked to areas of poverty and weak governance.</li><li>Women and children are more at risk of sexual exploitation.</li></ul>	The number of birth-related deaths in women per 100,000 live births, mainly due to limited access to safe healthcare services, poverty, and a lack of education. Patterns: <ul><li>According to WHO, in 2023 260,000 women died during pregnancy or childbirth.</li><li>Predominantly in issue in LIDCs and EDCs.</li><li>70% of deaths occurred in Sub-Saharan Africa</li><li>17% occurred in south Asia</li></ul>	The state-ordained killing of people as a form of punishment for committing a crime. Patterns: <ul><li>Most executions occurred in retentionist countries: China, Iran, Saudi Arabia, Somalia and the USA in certain states (2023).</li><li>Most of Europe have abolished the death penalty (abolitionists).</li><li>Political regimes are largely related to capital punishment.</li><li>An estimated 1153 executions took place in 2023 but it is likely many more occurred under state secrets.</li></ul>

Geography of gender inequality
- The United Nation's Gender Inequality Index (GII) uses three factors to measure inequality:
  - Reproductive health
  - Empowerment
  - The labour market
- GII is scored from 0–1, with a low score indicating low levels of inequality. As of 2023, countries with the highest levels of gender inequality include Yemen, Nigeria, and Afghanistan. Countries with the lowest levels of inequality include Norway, Denmark, and Sweden.
- Challenges related to gender inequality:
  - **Educational opportunities:**
    - Poorer families often can't afford education for all of their children, and it is normally son's education that is prioritised.
    - In many cultures, girls are expected to help within the household, marry early or have children at a young age meaning their educational opportunities are limited.
    - Lack of investment into resources and infrastructure to support girls' education such as sufficient toilet facilities.
    - Governments can ban female access to education. For example, since the Taliban takeover in 2021, secondary education is banned for girls in Afghanistan.
  - **Access to reproductive health services:**
    - Early/child marriage is linked to high-risk pregnancies among girls as they become excluded from education and access to healthcare is limited.
    - Providing education to girls and women relating to sexual and reproductive health can improve access to reproductive health and inform decisions on safe pregnancies and family planning.
    - Female genital mutilation (FGM) is an extremely harmful practice used in some cultures that can have devastating effects on women's reproductive health often causing chronic pain, infections and major complications during childbirth.
    - Sexual violence can impact women's reproductive health by increasing the risk of sexually transmitted infections and pregnancy, coupled with fear of seeking medical help.
  - **Employment opportunities:**
    - Discrimination in the workplace can prevent equal employment opportunities women can face abuse, unequal pay and limited career progression because of their gender.
    - Certain cultures, religions and social norms suggest that women should not work and that their role should be domestic in the household.
    - Affordable childcare is critical for women to access equal employment opportunities as a lack thereof often forces women to stay at home or not return to work.

Human rights

Only: OCR, Edexcel

Human rights violations as a consequence of conflict

How do human rights violations cause conflict?	How can human rights violations be a consequence of conflict?
• Discrimination based on ethnicity or religion for example can lead to wrongful imprisonment and genocide. • Restricting access to food, water, education and other human rights. • Restricting freedom of speech or the right to vote under an oppressive government.	• Mass displacement of people because of conflict and loss of homes causing an increase in refugees seeking safety. • Destruction of infrastructure that provides food, water, healthcare services, and education.

When human rights violations occur, geopolitical intervention often takes place to protect civilians and uphold international humanitarian law. The UN and other international organisations respond to conflicts through action shaped by the flow of these factors:
- **People:** large scale displacement of people impacted by conflict can cause geopolitical interventions. In return, humanitarian and aid workers are sent to conflict zones as part of peacekeeping missions.
- **Money:** governments, international organisations and NGOs send money in the form of aid or funding for peacekeeping missions for example.
- **Ideas:** the exchange of ideas is important in the response to human rights issues. Campaigns, media coverage and international conferences help to strengthen humanitarian law and spread awareness on country's human rights violations.
- **Technology:** advancing technology helps to monitor, document and intervene in human rights violations. Satellite imaging and drones for example help to monitor inaccessible regions or dangerous conflict zones.

Case study – human rights governance

	Syria

Global, national, and NGO interactions	• **UN (Independent Commission of Inquiry):** established by the Human Rights Council in August 2011 to document war crimes, war crimes, and crimes against humanity, providing over 20 reports and interviewing more than 11,000 witnesses.
	  ○ *National Commission for the Missing* (established May 2025), tasked with documenting disappearances.
	  ○ *National Commission for Transitional Justice* (also May 2025), mandated to address past violations and help victims.
	• **NGO (Syria Justice and Accountability Centre, SJAC):** a USA-based nonprofit that documents violations, collects evidence, monitors war crime trials (e.g. in Germany), assists in mass grave investigations, and develops data systems shared with international justice mechanisms – operations recently impacted by changes in USA foreign aid.

Consequences for local communities	• **Establishing truth and redress:** national commissions bring a domestic mechanism for victims to seek recognition, clarity, and perhaps reparations, filling a gap in justice capacity. • **Documentation and accountability:** SJAC's work supports prosecutions abroad, builds historical record, and empowers survivors and families.
Challenges and limitations	• Commissions have limited scope and face criticism for partiality. • UN efforts, while thorough in documentation, have struggled to translate findings into justice or outcomes on the ground.

Global governance of human rights

	Role
Institutions	Institutions help to maintain humanitarian law through multiple agencies such as the UN Human Rights Council (UNHRC) and the Office of the High Commissioner for Human Rights (OHCHR).
Treaties and laws	Treaties and laws create legally binding commitments for members to uphold human rights, in which the violation of these rights has consequences. For example, the Convention on the Elimination of All Forms of Discriminations Against Women (CEDAW) is a treaty developed to protect the rights of women.
NGOs	NGOs such as Amnesty work to promote human rights, raise awareness and support victims of violations within countries through monitoring and aid provision.

Consequences of global governance of human rights

Short term effects	Long term effects
• NGOs and other agencies often aim to provide immediate relief and aid to affected populations. This can be food, water, medicine or shelter for example. • Military protection from UN peacekeeping missions helps to protect vulnerable civilians from human rights violations and violence. • Military protection may also cause damage to infrastructure and a continued reliance on aid and support.	• Empowerment of marginalised groups such as equal rights for men and women. • Adaptation of laws to align with human rights treaties and international law. • Developments of fair courts and judicial systems as well as reduction is corruption and discrimination. • Better access to educational opportunities.